ASEAN CORPORATE GOVERNANCE SCORECARD COUNTRY REPORTS AND ASSESSMENTS 2019

ASIAN DEVELOPMENT BANK

ADB

Notes:
In this publication, "$" refers to United States dollars, unless otherwise stated.
The terms "publicly listed companies," "listed companies," and "companies" are used interchangeably in the report.

ADB recognizes "China" as the People's Republic of China and "Vietnam" as Viet Nam.

On the cover: Improved corporate governance standards are important for the growth of ASEAN capital markets and are being supported by ADB and the ASEAN Capital Markets Forum.

Cover design by Jasper Lauzon.

Contents

Tables and Figures

Tables

Figures

Foreword

By the Director General, Southeast Asia Department, Asian Development Bank

The impact of the coronavirus disease (COVID-19) pandemic on corporations and economies has been significant. Global gross domestic product (GDP) in 2020 saw a contraction of 3.3%. The pandemic created the worst recession since the Great Depression. In addition to the tragic loss of life, millions have lost jobs, income, and savings. Poverty and unemployment rates in many countries reversed from the progress gained in years before the pandemic. During this challenging time, corporate governance is important, especially for a company's resilience and recovery.

Recovery requires substantial financial resources especially through the capital markets. It is therefore necessary for corporate governance policies and frameworks to adapt so that existing and new companies can access the capital they need. It is equally important to keep a close eye on various aspects of corporate governance including the duties of the board of directors and disclosure to stakeholders. The ASEAN Corporate Governance Scorecard (ACGS) plays a critical role in addressing this need.

The ACGS is a joint initiative of the ASEAN Capital Market Forum (ACMF) and the Asian Development Bank (ADB) that was conceptualized in 2011, involving six participating countries (Indonesia, Malaysia, Philippines, Singapore, Thailand, and Viet Nam). The main objective of the ACGS is to raise the corporate governance standards of publicly listed companies and give greater international visibility to well-governed companies in members of the Association of Southeast Asian Nations (ASEAN). The ACGS has a robust assessment methodology. First, the domestic ranking body of each country assesses the corporate governance performances of publicly listed companies based on the criteria in the ACGS. This is then followed by a peer review process for consistency and quality control. One of the outputs of these assessments is the biennial ACGS report published as joint ADB-ACMF knowledge pieces. The report you have in your hand is the fifth of such publication.

We are pleased to note, as highlighted in this report, that corporate governance standards among ASEAN publicly listed companies have improved over the years. For example, the mean score of publicly listed companies assessed improved by 37.4% in 2019 compared to the first assessment in 2012. It is also heartening to note that the improvements in 2019 compared to 2017 have been observed in all six participating countries—with Viet Nam showing the most improvement, having a 32% increase in its score.

Overall, ASEAN-listed companies performed the best in Part C of the ACGS, on the "Role of Stakeholders." On the other hand, there is room for improvement in Part E on the "Responsibilities of the Board." This is a unique role of the ACGS assessments. It highlights ASEAN best practices while simultaneously also recommends areas for improvement. It serves as a useful guide for regulators and policy makers on areas to focus on.

ADB is honored to partner with the ACMF in this joint initiative, and our role over the years has also evolved. In the early years, ADB brought together regional corporate governance experts to develop the ACGS. This included funding some of the initial development work. Subsequently, as the ACGS became more sustainable, ADB's role focused on enhancing the credibility of the assessment and promoting the ACGS to the international community including investors. It has been a long and fruitful development journey. The ACGS is a testimony that differing levels of capital market development is not necessarily a barrier to regional integration initiative.

We would like to take this opportunity to thank the ACMF regulators and the domestic ranking bodies of each country for all the tireless effort in completing the assessments underpinning this report. Our special appreciation to the Securities and Exchange Commission of the Philippines for leading the ACGS initiative within the ACMF structure. To conclude, we pledge our support to the ACMF as it strives to achieve vision 2025 of being an inter-connected, inclusive, and resilient ASEAN capital market.

Ramesh Subramaniam
Director General, Southeast Asia Department, Asian Development Bank

Foreword

The ASEAN Corporate Governance Scorecard (ACGS) is the brainchild of a successful partnership between the ASEAN Capital Markets Forum (ACMF) and ADB. The scorecard is supported by a rigorous methodology developed to assess the corporate governance standing and performance of publicly listed companies (PLCs) in the six participating Association of Southeast Asian Nations (ASEAN) members: Indonesia, Malaysia, the Philippines, Singapore, Thailand, and Viet Nam.

At the outset, the presence of the ACGS sends a strong message to the world that the ASEAN places corporate governance at the top of its priorities. Nine years after it was first launched in 2011, the ACGS has evolved to become a strong driver of corporate governance reforms among PLCs. More importantly, the ACGS is now widely used by capital market regulators, investors, fund managers, and other stakeholders as a reliable reference document to get a better picture of the corporate governance climate in each of the participating ASEAN Member Countries and across the ASEAN region. The ACGS has indeed come a long way since its inception, but there is no doubt that the challenges are far from over.

The recent developments surrounding the global pandemic have made it clear now more than ever that good corporate governance plays an indispensable role in keeping the global economy resilient. The current situation forced all countries to implement extraordinary measures, which placed effective risk management and crisis response at the forefront, spelling the difference between survival and closure among corporations. In these difficult times, the call for good corporate governance has become an urgent matter that transcends prestige, social, and political borders, and the ACGS itself.

This notwithstanding, we must not lose sight of what this exercise is all about. The ACGS was created to highlight the spectacular work done by our esteemed PLCs and boost foreign capital infusion in the ASEAN region. We take pride in the fact that this initiative has become an avenue for recognizing the valiant efforts of each and every PLC awardee and the corporate governance champions rallying behind them. Know that your contributions have inspired us to continuously find ways in which we can make this initiative better than it was in previous years.

The ASEAN Corporate Governance Scorecard Country Reports and Assessments 2019 that you have in your hands today is a product of the tireless work of the domestic ranking bodies in the region, and their respective corporate governance experts. We hope that this publication expands its reach and encourages other ASEAN members to participate in, and contribute to, this initiative. Let this publication be a testament that regional integration is the key to overcoming political, economic, and cultural differences, building better diplomatic relations and encouraging cooperation among countries.

As the Chair of the ASEAN Corporate Governance Working Group, it is my pleasure to witness the growth of the participating ASEAN Member Countries at the local and regional level. Through this initiative, regional cooperation among the participating ASEAN members has become stronger and more focused toward the goal of branding the region as an asset class based on corporate governance.

Finally, I would like to acknowledge the ACMF, the Asian Development Bank, and our national regulators, who have been encouraging and resolute in their support throughout this whole journey. The group is very fortunate to have worked with visionaries who have nothing but the region's best interests in mind. The ACGS Working Group, currently led by the Philippine Securities and Exchange Commission, remains committed to raise corporate governance standards in the ASEAN region with the aim of propelling the economy past this global pandemic and helping the capital market regain its momentum. On this note, the Philippine Securities and Exchange Commission pledges its absolute support to the ACGS initiative as its partner today and in the years to come.

Emilio B. Aquino

Chair, ASEAN Corporate Governance Working Group

Acknowledgments

This report was prepared by a group of Association of Southeast Asian Nations (ASEAN) corporate governance experts composed of Angela Simatupang (RSM Indonesia), Devanesan Evanson (Minority Shareholders Watch Group, Malaysia), Leonardo Jose M. Berba (Institute of Corporate Directors, Philippines), John Lim (Singapore Institute of Directors and the Centre for Governance and Sustainability of the National University of Singapore Business School), Kulvech Janvatanavit (Thai Institute of Directors), and Thinh Viet Nguyen and Hien Thu Nguyen (Viet Nam Institute of Directors). The ADB and the Philippines Securities and Exchange Commission jointly led the publication of this report.

In Viet Nam, the project could not have been completed without the important guidance of the State Securities Commission of Vietnam, the Chair of the Board of Directors of the Vietnam Institute of Directors (VIOD), Ha Thu Thanh, and the VIOD Executive Board. The project was conducted in Viet Nam with the continuous financial support of the International Finance Corporation (IFC) since 2015, in partnership with Swiss Economic Cooperation (SECO). In 2019–2020, for the first time, the project in Viet Nam was co-supported by VIOD and IFC in partnership with SECO and the Government of Japan.

The ASEAN Corporate Governance Scorecard is an initiative under the ASEAN Capital Markets Forum. The ASEAN Capital Markets Forum endorsed the scorecard and the methodology used in the ranking exercise but was not involved in the assessment and selection of the publicly listed companies in the sample.

Executive Summary

The Association of Southeast Asian Nations (ASEAN) Corporate Governance Initiative, composed of the ASEAN Corporate Governance Scorecard and assessment and ranking of ASEAN publicly listed companies (PLCs), is among several regional initiatives of the ASEAN Capital Markets Forum (ACMF). This initiative has been a collaborative effort of ACMF and ADB since 2011.

The ACMF Working Group D, the body responsible for this initiative, is currently led by the Philippines Securities and Exchange Commission after the handover from Securities Commission Malaysia in November 2015. Its members include capital market regulators and corporate governance proponents from the region. The ASEAN Scorecard was developed and is continuously improved based on international benchmarks such as the Organisation for Economic Co-operation and Development (OECD) Principles of Corporate Governance (2004), G20/OECD Principles of Corporate Governance (2015), International Corporate Governance Network (ICGN) Corporate Governance Principles, as well as industry-leading practices from ASEAN and the world.

The first three editions of the annual ASEAN Corporate Governance Scorecard: Country Reports and Assessments provided the impetus in raising public awareness on this initiative and in profiling the top domestic PLCs from each participating country. The fourth edition of the ASEAN Corporate Governance Scorecard: Country Reports and Assessments continued the momentum toward elevating the visibility of ASEAN PLCs among investors. The fifth edition of the report presents the results of the 2019 assessment. It comes after an assessment hiatus of 1 year wherein in 2016 the Working Group focused on a holistic and thorough review of the scorecard and its methodology to ensure that it continues to be aligned with and prescribes internationally recognized best standards and is contextualized based on the current need of the ASEAN Market and its PLCs. The new scorecard became the basis of both the 2017 and 2019 assessments.

For this round, ASEAN corporate governance experts from the domestic ranking bodies (DRBs) of Indonesia, Malaysia, the Philippines, Singapore, Thailand, and Viet Nam undertook the corporate governance assessment of ASEAN PLCs. The process concluded in April 2020 with the awarding done virtually in November 2020. The DRBs were (i) RSM Indonesia; (ii) Minority Shareholders Watch Group, Malaysia; (iii) Institute of Corporate Directors, Philippines; (iv) Singapore Institute of Directors and the Centre for Governance and Sustainability of the National University of Singapore Business School; (v) Thai Institute of Directors; and (vi) Viet Nam Institute of Directors.

2016 Holistic Review of the ASEAN Corporate Governance Scorecard

After five rounds of assessment, it was decided that no assessment would be held in 2016. Rather, the corporate governance experts from the participating countries were tasked to conduct a holistic and comprehensive review of the scorecard to respond to the updated principles and recommendations of the G20/OECD Principles of Corporate Governance and to take into consideration increased investor expectations and developments in business and corporate governance practices. The review was completed in early 2017 and the new scorecard was launched during the ACMF Chairs' Meeting on 13 March 2017. Following the review of the scorecard, the ACGS was to be conducted biennially. The revised scorecard was used in the 2017 and 2019 assessments.

The key revisions in the scorecard include the following: (1) the addition of new items reflecting the G20/OECD Principles of Corporate Governance; (2) additional weightage for the Role of Stakeholders section and for questions recognized as higher corporate governance standards; (3) streamlining of questions for a more coherent scorecard; and (4) introducing an independent validation in addition to the existing domestic and peer review process, although the validation was conducted only during the 2017 assessment. The enhancements were introduced to strengthen the quality of assessment and to expand insights on corporate governance practices of companies from the participating countries. A summary of the changes in the scorecard is provided in Table 1.1.

Table 1.1: Summary of Changes in the ASEAN Corporate Governance Scorecard

PART	ACGS v.1 No. of Items	ACGS v.2 No. of Items	ACGS v.1 Weightage	ACGS v.2 Weightage
A—Rights of Shareholders	25	21	10%	10%
B—Equitable Treatment of Shareholders	18	15	15%	10%
C—Role of Stakeholders	21	13	**10%**	**15%**
D—Disclosure and Transparency	41	32	25%	25%
E—Responsibilities of the Board	74	65	40%	40%
Level 1 Total	**179**	**146**	**100%**	**100%**
Bonus	11	13	26	30
Penalties	22	25	(59)	(67)

( ) = negative.
Source: ACMF Working Group D Secretariat 2019.

Overview of the Revised ASEAN Corporate Governance Scorecard

The G20/OECD Principles of Corporate Governance were used as the main benchmark for the ASEAN Scorecard. Many of the items in the scorecard are international and regional best practices that may go beyond the requirements of national legislation.

The ASEAN corporate governance experts also drew from the existing body of work and ranking initiatives in the region, including those of institutes of directors, shareholder associations, and universities, to guide the initial inclusion of items in the ASEAN Scorecard.

The revised scorecard continues to cover the following five areas of the OECD principles:
(i)   Part A: Rights of Shareholders,
(ii)   Part B: Equitable Treatment of Shareholders,
(iii)   Part C: Role of Stakeholders,
(iv)   Part D: Disclosure and Transparency, and
(v)   Part E: Responsibilities of the Board.

The scorecard uses two levels of scoring designed to better capture the actual implementation of the substance of good corporate governance. Level 1 comprises descriptors or items that are, in essence, indicative of (i) the laws, rules, regulations, and requirements of each ASEAN member country; and (ii) basic expectations of the G20/OECD principles. Level 2 consists of (i) bonus items reflecting other emerging good practices and (ii) penalty items reflecting actions and events that are indicative of poor governance.

Following the 2016 review of the scorecard, (1) the percentage of Part C on the Role of Stakeholders increased from 10% to 15%; (2) the questions were streamlined resulting in a decrease in the total number of questions from 179 to 146; (3) 31 questions were also given more weight; and (4) adjustments were made on the bonus and penalty sections, giving more points for exceptional governance practices and greater penalty for governance violations. The review resulted in the maximum attainable score increasing from 126 points in 2015 to 130 points for the 2017 and 2019 assessment years (Table 2.1).

Table 2.1:   Comparison of Question Numbers and Scores (2012, 2013, 2014, 2015, 2017, and 2019)

		Number of Questions					
		2012	2013	2014	2015	2017	2019
Level 1	Part A	26 [10]	25 [10]	25 [10]	25 [10]	21 [10]	21 [10]
	Part B	17 [15]	17 [15]	17 [15]	18 [15]	15 [10]	15 [10]
	Part C	21 [10]	21 [10]	21 [10]	21 [10]	13 [15]	13 [15]
	Part D	42 [25]	40 [25]	41 [25]	41 [25]	32 [25]	32 [25]
	Part E	79 [40]	76 [40]	75 [40]	74 [40]	65 [40]	65 [40]
Level 2	Bonus	11 [17]	9 [42]	11 [28]	11 [26]	13 [30]	13 [30]
	Penalty	23 [(90)]	21 [(53)]	21 [(50)]	22 [(59)]	25 [(67)]	25 [(67)]

( ) = negative.
Note: Numbers in brackets denote maximum attainable scores for each part; however, for the penalty section, numbers in brackets denote maximum deductible scores.
Source: ACMF Working Group D Secretariat 2019.

Level 1

Level 1 consists of 146 items and is divided into 5 parts corresponding to the respective OECD principles. Each part carries a different weight in relation to the Level 1 total score of 100 points based on the relative importance of the area. The composition and structure of Level 1 are provided in Table 2.2.

Table 2.2:   Composition and Structure of Level 1

Level 1	Number of Questions	Weight (% of total Level 1 score)	Maximum Attainable Score
Part A: Rights of Shareholders	21	10	10 points
Part B: Equitable Treatment of Shareholders	15	10	10 points
Part C: Role of Stakeholders	13	15	15 points
Part D: Disclosure and Transparency	32	25	25 points
Part E: Responsibilities of the Board	65	40	40 points

Source: ACMF Working Group D Secretariat 2019.

The weighted score of each part is obtained using the following formula:

$$\text{Score} = \frac{\text{total points scored by PLCs}}{\text{total possible points from all questions}} \times \text{weightage for the part (in points)}$$

The total number of questions is computed after adjusting for items that are not applicable for a PLC.

As an example, if PLC1 scores in 19 out of the 20 items in part A, then:

$$\text{PLC1's score in Part A} = \frac{19}{20} \times 10 \text{ points} = 9.5 \text{ points}$$

The Level 1 score is obtained by totaling the scores for Parts A through E in Level 1. The maximum attainable score for Level 1 is therefore 100 points.

Hence, if PLC1 scores 9.5 points in part A and perfect in each of Parts B through E in Level 1, then

$$\text{PLC1's Level 1 score} = 9.5 + 10 + 15 + 25 + 40 = 99.5 \text{ points}$$

Level 2

Level 2 consists of bonus and penalty items that are meant to enhance the robustness of the ASEAN Scorecard in assessing the extent to which companies apply the spirit of good corporate governance. The purpose of the bonus items is to recognize companies that go beyond the items in Level 1 by adopting other emerging good corporate governance practices. The penalty items are designed to downgrade companies with poor corporate governance practices that are not reflected in their scores for Level 1, such as being sanctioned by regulators for breaches of listing rules.

Level 2 contains 13 bonus and 26 penalty items, each with a different number of points. The maximum attainable bonus points are 30 while the maximum deductible penalty is 67 (Table 2.3).

Table 2.3:   Composition and Structure of Level 2

Level 2	Number of Questions	Maximum Score (points)
Bonus	13	30
Penalty	25	(67)

( ) = negative.
Source: ACMF Working Group D Secretariat 2019.

The Level 2 score is obtained by totaling the bonus and penalty scores. For example, if PLC1 scores 26 bonus points and 3 penalty points, then

$$\text{PLC1's Level 2 score} = 26 + (-3) = 23 \text{ points}$$

Total Score

The total score is obtained using the following formula:

$$\text{Total score} = \text{Level 1 score} + \text{Level 2 score}$$

To illustrate, PLC1's total score = 99.5 + 23 = 122.5 points.

The maximum attainable score is 130 points (100 points from Level 1 and 30 points from Level 2).

Default Items

Default items are accorded when a country has specific legislation or requirements that will enable all domestic companies assessed to automatically score a point for a particular item. The company is considered to have adopted the practice unless there is evidence to the contrary. To ensure a transparent process, all countries must disclose their default items before the assessment process begins.

Assessment Methodology

The assessments on corporate governance standards of PLCs were based on publicly available and accessible information such as annual reports, corporate websites, notices, circulars, articles of association, minutes of shareholder meetings, corporate governance policies, codes of conduct, and sustainability reports. For a company to be assessed and ranked, most of the available documents must be in English. To be given points on the scorecard, all disclosures must be unambiguous and sufficiently complete.

The scorecard assessment methodology previously only involved two processes: the domestic assessment and the peer review process. In the 2017 assessment, a third process was added—an independent external validation. The 2019 assessment did not include an external validation.

Domestic Assessment Process

The domestic assessment is the first stage of the assessment process. Using the scorecard, the DRBs in the participating countries assess the corporate governance practices of their top 100 domestic PLCs based on market capitalization.

Peer Review Process

The peer review process differentiates this exercise from other types of corporate governance assessments. To conduct the peer review, the top 35 PLCs in each country, ranked according to their total scores in the preliminary assessments, were subjected to peer review by the other DRBs. Peer reviewers were assigned randomly for each PLC, ensuring that DRBs had the opportunity to assess PLCs from all the other countries. This step was incorporated in the assessment process as a measure to validate and confirm the assessment by the DRB and to ensure consistency in the interpretation of questions in the scorecard.

During this process, DRBs and peer reviewers carried out engagements and discussions to reconcile any differences in their scores and to agree on a final score for each PLC. Where the discussions revealed any systemic differences in the DRBs' assessment from that finally agreed due to interpretation of questions, the DRB would then have to apply the revision in interpretation and reassess across all the PLCs, including those that had not been subjected to peer review. This check and balance process improved accuracy of results.

Independent External Validation for the 2017 Assessment

An independent external validation was introduced as a third process during the 2017 assessment to further improve the robustness of the assessment process. The primary objectives of the process were to check alignment between the corporate governance practices disclosed by the PLCs and those in actual practice and to check the dynamics of the board and key company stakeholders to determine their commitment to high standards of corporate governance. Only the top 70 ASEAN PLCs were subjected to the validation process in 2017. Validation was conducted by KPMG Singapore through company interviews focused on five key areas: (1) strategy; (2) board composition; (3) board evaluation; (4) remuneration (executive directors/chief executive officer); and (5) risk management and internal controls.

As stated above, the 2019 assessment did not include the process of external validation; however, the working group is considering the possibility of including this process in subsequent assessments, subject to the approval of the ACMF.

Overall Results and Analysis

For the 2019 assessment, a total of 582 PLCs were assessed. The number of PLCs assessed was not equally distributed given the limited availability of company disclosures in English in Viet Nam, which resulted in having less than 100 of its domestic PLCs being assessed (Figure 2.1).

Figure 2.1:   Number of Publicly Listed Companies Assessed by Country, 2019

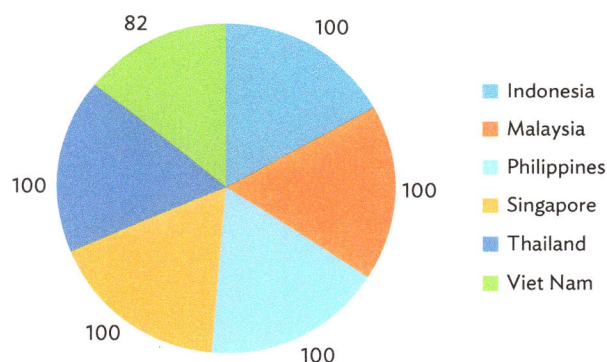

Legend:
- Indonesia
- Malaysia
- Philippines
- Singapore
- Thailand
- Viet Nam

Source: ACMF Working Group D Secretariat 2019.

In the 2019 assessment round, around 57% of the PLCs assessed had market capitalization of at least $1 billion (Figure 2.2). The average size of PLCs was $3.32 billion, with the largest having a market capitalization of $47.65 billion, and the smallest with $39.8 million.

Figure 2.2:   Distribution of Publicly Listed Companies Based on Market Capitalization, 2019

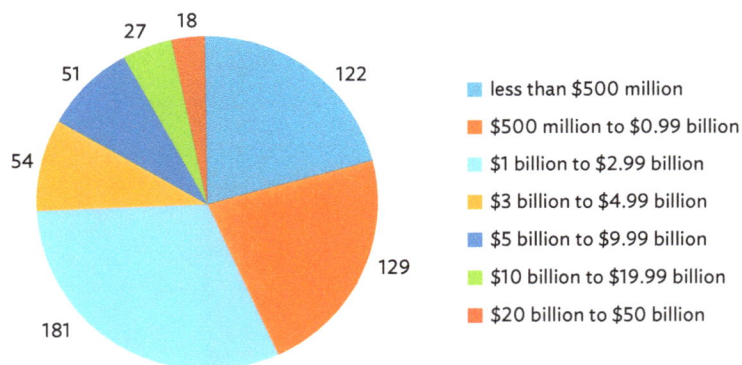

- less than $500 million
- $500 million to $0.99 billion
- $1 billion to $2.99 billion
- $3 billion to $4.99 billion
- $5 billion to $9.99 billion
- $10 billion to $19.99 billion
- $20 billion to $50 billion

Source: ACMF Working Group D Secretariat 2019.

The mean total score increased in 2019 to 81.21 compared to 72.57 points in 2017, or an increase of 12% on the previous assessment (Table 2.4).

Table 2.4:   Comparison of Total Scores, 2012–2015, 2017, and 2019
(points)

	2012	2013	2014	2015	2017	2019
Mean	53.66	64.02	67.69	71.81	72.57	81.21
Median	55.79	64.55	68.29	72.69	72.30	84.58
Maximum Attainable Score	117	142	128	126	130	130

Source: ACMF Working Group D Secretariat 2019.

For Level 1 (i.e., excluding Level 2 bonus and penalty scores), the mean score in the 2019 assessment was 74.65 points, 7.8% higher than the mean score of 69.25 in the 2017 assessment. Although there was minimal improvement in the Level 1 score compared to the last assessment, the overall increase of 37.43% since 2012 indicates the significant improvement in fundamental and core corporate governance practices for the ASEAN PLCs (Table 2.5).

Table 2.5:   Comparison of Level 1 Scores, 2012–2015, 2017, and 2019
(points)

	2012	2013	2014	2015	2017	2019
Mean	54.32	60.09	64.72	68.87	69.25	74.65
Median	56.91	61.50	65.56	70.16	70.90	77.59
Maximum Attainable Score	100	100	100	100	100	100

Source: ACMF Working Group D Secretariat 2019.

With respect to Level 2, the mean score in the 2019 assessment almost doubled to 6.57 points from 3.32 points, an increase of 97.89%. (Table 2.6).

Table 2.6:   Comparison of Level 2 Scores, 2012–2015, 2017, and 2019
(points)

	2012	2013	2014	2015	2017	2019
Mean	(0.66)	3.92	2.98	2.94	3.32	6.57
Median	0	3.00	2.00	2.00	2.00	6.00
Maximum Attainable Score	17	42	28	26	30	30

( ) = negative.
Source: ACMF Working Group D Secretariat 2019.

The 2019 scores of ASEAN companies positively moved toward the upper scale in achieving maximum attainable scores (Figure 2.3). The highest score obtained in 2019 was 129.46 points, roughly a half-point short of the maximum attainable score. In addition, the number of ASEAN companies scoring 100 points and above increased by 71%, from 66 companies in 2017 to 113 companies in 2019 (Figure 2.3).

Figure 2.3:   Distribution of Total Scores, 2019

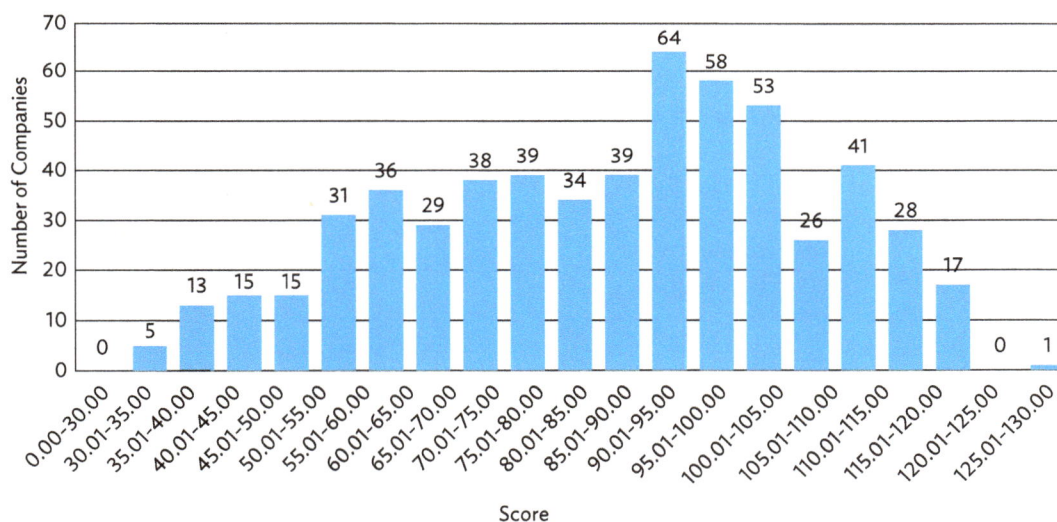

Source: ACMF Working Group D Secretariat 2019.

All ASEAN countries' mean scores in 2019 increased from the previous assessment in 2017. Thailand continued to be the overall best performer with the highest mean score among all participating countries, followed closely by Malaysia in second place, with Singapore coming in third (Figure 2.4). Viet Nam showed the most improvement from the previous assessment, having a 32% increase in its score from 2017 to 2019.

When the results were analyzed according to the various areas of corporate governance (Figure 2.5), Thailand scored the highest mean for Parts A, B, C, and D in Level 1, while Malaysia scored highest in Part E.

Overall, ASEAN listed companies performed the best with respect to Part C (Role of Stakeholders), with 203 companies garnering the maximum attainable score.

Figure 2.4:   Mean Scores by Country

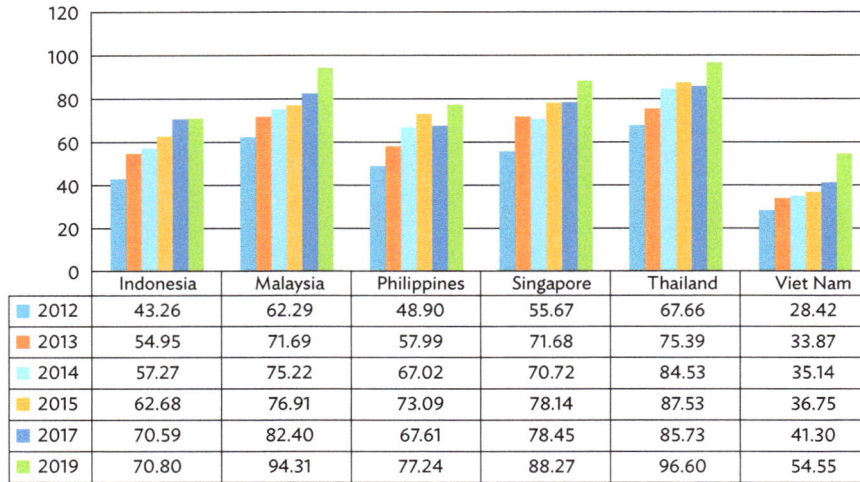

	Indonesia	Malaysia	Philippines	Singapore	Thailand	Viet Nam
2012	43.26	62.29	48.90	55.67	67.66	28.42
2013	54.95	71.69	57.99	71.68	75.39	33.87
2014	57.27	75.22	67.02	70.72	84.53	35.14
2015	62.68	76.91	73.09	78.14	87.53	36.75
2017	70.59	82.40	67.61	78.45	85.73	41.30
2019	70.80	94.31	77.24	88.27	96.60	54.55

Source: ACMF Working Group D Secretariat 2019.

Figure 2.5:   Level 1 Scores by Part

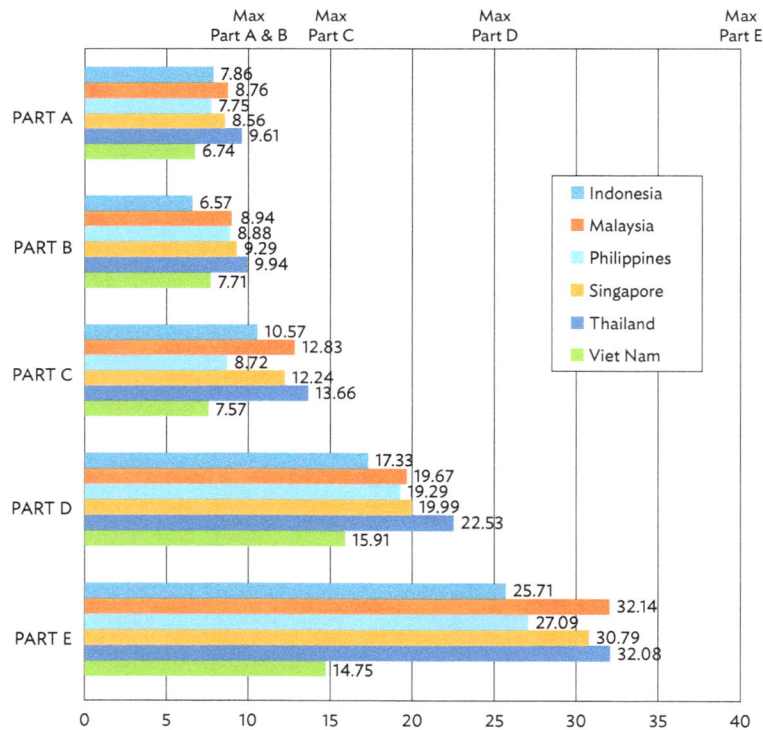

Note: Part A, Rights of Shareholders; Part B, Equitable Treatment of Shareholders; Part C, Role of Stakeholders; Part D, Disclosure and Transparency; and Part E, Responsibilities of the Board.

Source: ACMF Working Group D Secretariat 2019.

2019 ASEAN Corporate Governance Scorecard Awards

The 2019 ASEAN Corporate Governance Scorecard Awards based on the 2019 assessment were announced in December 2020, with the Viet Nam Institute of Directors as the organizer with the support of the State Securities Commission of Viet Nam.

For the 2019 assessment year, there were three categories of awards: (a) Top 20 ASEAN PLCs, (b) ASEAN Asset Class, and (c) Top 3 PLCs per country. Due to the COVID-19 pandemic, the working group decided to cancel the holding of a physical awarding event. Instead, certificates will be issued for each category of award and the names and logos of the companies will appear in a booklet that will be posted on the website of the ACMF and ADB.

Out of the Top 20 ASEAN PLCs for the 2019 assessment, Malaysia had the greatest number of companies with seven. Singapore followed with five companies, while Thailand and the Philippines each had four companies (Table 3.1).

A total of 135 ASEAN companies qualified for the ASEAN Asset Class award. This award is given to ASEAN PLCs that attained a final score of 97.5 and above (i.e., at least 75% of the maximum attainable score of 130). Thailand had the greatest number of awardee companies at 42, followed by Malaysia at a close second with 37 companies and Singapore in third place with 26 companies (Table 3.1).

Table 3.1:   Distribution of Companies in ASEAN Top 20
and ASEAN Asset Class per Country, 2019

	Top 20 ASEAN	ASEAN Asset Class
Indonesia	0	10
Malaysia	7	37
Philippines	4	19
Singapore	5	26
Thailand	4	42
Viet Nam	0	1
TOTAL	20	135

Source: ACMF Working Group D Secretariat 2019.

The ASEAN Asset Class awardees comprise a diverse mix of companies coming from the finance, industry, consumer goods and services, property, energy, and telecommunications and media sectors, among others. Their total mean score was 107.45. However, the Top 20 ASEAN PLCs, which are clearly set on adopting the best corporate governance practices and setting high standards for the other ASEAN PLCs to follow, had a total mean score of 117.98, which was 9.8% higher than the mean score of the ASEAN Asset Class PLCs.

In addition to the Top 20 ASEAN and ASEAN Asset Class award, the achievements of the Top 3 companies per country are also recognized.

Conclusion

The 2019 assessment, together with the 2017 assessment, bears the results of the holistic and comprehensive review of the scorecard and its methodology in 2016. Although the revised scorecard had stricter guidelines, the mean score of the ASEAN PLCs still increased compared to previous assessments. Also noteworthy is the increase in mean scores of assessed PLCs in all participating countries from 2017 to the current 2019 assessment. The number of ASEAN companies exceeding 100 points likewise increased significantly. This highlights the consistent improvement in the corporate governance practices of the top PLCs in the ASEAN region. However, the challenge is to encourage the lower ranked PLCs to improve their performance and further increase the mean scores of all PLCs across the region and, consequently, to promote inclusivity and further achieve the scorecard's objective of promoting ASEAN PLCs as investable companies and ASEAN as an asset class.

Table 3.2: Top 20 ASEAN Publicly Listed Companies
(in alphabetical order)

No.	Company Name	Country
1	AMMB HOLDINGS BHD	Malaysia
2	AXIATA GROUP BERHAD	Malaysia
3	AYALA LAND, INC.	Philippines
4	BANGCHAK CORPORATION PUBLIC COMPANY LIMITED	Thailand
5	BURSA MALAYSIA BHD	Malaysia
6	CHINA BANKING CORPORATION	Philippines
7	CIMB GROUP HOLDINGS BERHAD	Malaysia
8	GLOBE TELECOM, INC.	Philippines
9	MALAYAN BANKING BHD	Malaysia
10	OVERSEA-CHINESE BANKING CORP LTD	Singapore
11	PETRONAS DAGANGAN BHD	Malaysia
12	PTT EXPLORATION AND PRODUCTION PUBLIC COMPANY LIMITED	Thailand
13	PTT PUBLIC COMPANY LIMITED	Thailand
14	RHB BANK BERHAD	Malaysia
15	SATS LTD	Singapore
16	SINGAPORE EXCHANGE LTD	Singapore
17	SINGAPORE TELECOMMUNICATIONS LTD	Singapore
18	SM PRIME HOLDINGS, INC.	Philippines
19	THAI OIL PUBLIC COMPANY LIMITED	Thailand
20	UNITED OVERSEAS BANK LTD	Singapore

Source: ACMF Working Group D Secretariat 2019.

Table 3.3: ASEAN Asset Class
(in alphabetical order)

No.	Company Name	Country
1	2GO GROUP, INC.	Philippines
2	ADVANCE INFO SERVICE PUBLIC COMPANY LIMITED	Thailand
3	AIRPORTS OF THAILAND PUBLIC COMPANY LIMITED	Thailand
4	ALLIANCE BANK MALAYSIA BERHAD	Malaysia
5	ALLIANZ MALAYSIA BHD	Malaysia
6	AMATA CORPORATION PUBLIC COMPANY LIMITED	Thailand
7	AMMB HOLDINGS BHD	Malaysia
8	ASTRO MALAYSIA HOLDINGS BERHAD	Malaysia
9	AXIATA GROUP BERHAD	Malaysia
10	AYALA CORPORATION	Philippines
11	AYALA LAND, INC.	Philippines
12	BANGCHAK CORPORATION PUBLIC COMPANY LIMITED	Thailand
13	BANGKOK AVIATION FUEL SERVICES PUBLIC COMPANY LIMITED	Thailand
14	BANK OF AYUDHYA PUBLIC COMPANY LIMITED	Thailand
15	BANK OF THE PHILIPPINE ISLANDS	Philippines
16	BDO UNIBANK, INC.	Philippines
17	BELLE CORPORATION	Philippines
18	BIMB HOLDINGS BHD	Malaysia
19	BRITISH AMERICAN TOBACCO (M) BHD	Malaysia
20	BURSA MALAYSIA BHD	Malaysia
21	CAHYA MATA SARAWAK BHD	Malaysia
22	CAPITALAND LTD.	Singapore
23	CENTRAL PATTANA PUBLIC COMPANY LIMITED	Thailand
24	CHAROEN POKPHAND FOODS PUBLIC COMPANY LIMITED	Thailand
25	CHINA BANKING CORPORATION	Philippines
26	CIMB GROUP HOLDINGS BERHAD	Malaysia
27	CITY DEVELOPMENTS LTD	Singapore
28	COL PUBLIC COMPANY LIMITED	Thailand
29	COMFORTDELGRO CORP LTD	Singapore
30	DBS GROUP HOLDINGS LTD	Singapore
31	DIGI.COM BHD	Malaysia
32	DMCI HOLDING, INC.	Philippines
33	EASTERN WATER RESOURCES DEVELOPMENT AND MANAGEMENT PCL.	Thailand
34	ELECTRICITY GENERATING PUBLIC COMPANY LIMITED	Thailand
35	FAR EAST ORCHARD LTD	Singapore
36	FRASER AND NEAVE LTD	Singapore
37	FRASERS CENTREPOINT LTD	Singapore
38	GLOBAL POWER SYNERGY PUBLIC COMPANY LIMITED	Thailand
39	GLOBE TELECOM, INC.	Philippines
40	GREAT EASTERN HOLDINGS LTD	Singapore

continued on next page

Table 3.3: ASEAN Asset Class (*continued*)

No.	Company Name	Country
41	GT CAPITAL HOLDINGS, INC.	Philippines
42	GUNKUL ENGINEERING PUBLIC COMPANY LIMITED	Thailand
43	HANA MICROELECTRONICS PUBLIC COMPANY LIMITED	Thailand
44	HOME PRODUCT CENTER PUBLIC COMPANY LIMITED	Thailand
45	HONG LEONG ASIA LIMITED	Singapore
46	IHH HEALTHCARE BERHAD	Malaysia
47	IJM CORPORATION BHD	Malaysia
48	INDORAMA VENTURES PUBLIC COMPANY LIMITED	Thailand
49	INTOUCH HOLDINGS PUBLIC COMPANY LIMITED	Thailand
50	IRPC PUBLIC COMPANY LIMITED	Thailand
51	KASIKORNBANK PUBLIC COMPANY LIMITED	Thailand
52	KCE ELECTRONICS PUBLIC COMPANY LIMITED	Thailand
53	KEPPEL CORP LTD	Singapore
54	KIATNAKIN BANK PUBLIC COMPANY LIMITED	Thailand
55	KRUNG THAI BANK PUBLIC COMPANY LIMITED	Thailand
56	KRUNGTHAI CARD PUBLIC COMPANY LIMITED	Thailand
57	LH FINANCIAL GROUP PUBLIC COMPANY LIMITED	Thailand
58	LPI CAPITAL BHD	Malaysia
59	MALAYAN BANKING BHD	Malaysia
60	MALAYSIA AIRPORTS HOLDINGS BHD	Malaysia
61	MALAYSIA BUILDING SOCIETY BHD	Malaysia
62	MALAYSIAN RESOURCES CORPORATION BERHAD	Malaysia
63	MANILA ELECTRIC COMPANY	Philippines
64	MEGAWIDE CONSTRUCTION CORPORATION	Philippines
65	METROPOLITAN BANK AND TRUST COMPANY	Philippines
66	MINOR INTERNATIONAL PUBLIC COMPANY LIMITED	Thailand
67	MUANGTHAI CAPITAL PUBLIC COMPANY LIMITED	Thailand
68	OLAM INTERNATIONAL LTD	Singapore
69	OVERSEA-CHINESE BANKING CORP LTD	Singapore
70	PERENNIAL REAL ESTATE HOLDINGS LTD	Singapore
71	PETRONAS CHEMICALS GROUP BHD	Malaysia
72	PETRONAS DAGANGAN BHD	Malaysia
73	PETRONAS GAS BHD	Malaysia
74	PHILIPPINE NATIONAL BANK	Philippines
75	PLAN B MEDIA PUBLIC COMPANY LIMITED	Thailand
76	PLDT, INC.	Philippines
77	PRECIOUS SHIPPING PUBLIC COMPANY LIMITED	Thailand
78	PREMIUM LEISURE CORPORATION	Philippines
79	PRUKSA HOLDING PUBLIC COMPANY LIMITED	Thailand
80	PT ANEKA TAMBANG TBK.	Indonesia
81	PT BANK CENTRAL ASIA TBK.	Indonesia
82	PT BANK CIMB NIAGA TBK.	Indonesia
83	PT BANK MANDIRI (PERSERO) TBK.	Indonesia

Table 3.3:   ASEAN Asset Class (*continued*)

No.	Company Name	Country
84	PT BANK MAYBANK INDONESIA TBK.	Indonesia
85	PT BANK PERMATA TBK.	Indonesia
86	PT BANK RAKYAT INDONESIA (PERSERO) TBK.	Indonesia
87	PT BANK TABUNGAN NEGARA (PERSERO) TBK.	Indonesia
88	PT JASA MARGA (PERSERO) TBK.	Indonesia
89	PT XL AXIATA TBK.	Indonesia
90	PTT EXPLORATION AND PRODUCTION PUBLIC COMPANY LIMITED	Thailand
91	PTT GLOBAL CHEMICAL PUBLIC COMPANY LIMITED	Thailand
92	PTT PUBLIC COMPANY LIMITED	Thailand
93	PUBLIC BANK BHD	Malaysia
94	RATCH GROUP PUBLIC COMPANY LIMITED	Thailand
95	RHB BANK BERHAD	Malaysia
96	SATS LTD	Singapore
97	SBS TRANSIT LTD	Singapore
98	SEMBCORP INDUSTRIES LTD	Singapore
99	SEMBCORP MARINE LTD	Singapore
100	SEMIRARA MINING AND POWER CORPORATION	Philippines
101	SIA ENGINEERING CO LTD	Singapore
102	SIME DARBY BHD	Malaysia
103	SIME DARBY PLANTATION BERHAD	Malaysia
104	SIME DARBY PROPERTY BERHAD	Malaysia
105	SINGAPORE AIRLINES LTD	Singapore
106	SINGAPORE EXCHANGE LTD	Singapore
107	SINGAPORE POST LTD	Singapore
108	SINGAPORE PRESS HOLDINGS LTD	Singapore
109	SINGAPORE TECHNOLOGIES ENGINEERING LTD	Singapore
110	SINGAPORE TELECOMMUNICATIONS LTD	Singapore
111	SINGHA ESTATE PUBLIC COMPANY LIMITED	Thailand
112	SM INVESTMENTS CORPORATION	Philippines
113	SM PRIME HOLDINGS, INC.	Philippines
114	S P SETIA BHD	Malaysia
115	STARHUB LTD	Singapore
116	SUNWAY BERHAD	Malaysia
117	SUNWAY CONSTRUCTION GROUP BERHAD	Malaysia
118	TELEKOM MALAYSIA BHD	Malaysia
119	TENAGA NASIONAL BHD	Malaysia
120	THAI AIRWAYS INTERNATIONAL PUBLIC COMPANY LIMITED	Thailand
121	THAI OIL PUBLIC COMPANY LIMITED	Thailand
122	THAI VEGETABLE OIL PUBLIC COMPANY LIMITED	Thailand
123	THE SIAM CEMENT PUBLIC COMPANY LIMITED	Thailand
124	THE SIAM COMMERCIAL BANK PUBLIC COMPANY LIMITED	Thailand
125	TISCO FINANCIAL GROUP PUBLIC COMPANY LIMITED	Thailand
126	TOA PAINT (THAILAND) PUBLIC COMPANY LIMITED	Thailand

continued on next page

Table 3.3:   **ASEAN Asset Class** (*continued*)

No.	Company Name	Country
127	TOP GLOVE CORPORATION BHD	Malaysia
128	TOTAL ACCESS COMMUNICATION PUBLIC COMPANY LIMITED	Thailand
129	UEM SUNRISE BERHAD	Malaysia
130	UMW HOLDINGS BHD	Malaysia
131	UNITED OVERSEAS BANK LTD	Singapore
132	VELESTO ENERGY BERHAD	Malaysia
133	VIET NAM DAIRY PRODUCTS JOINT STOCK COMPANY	Viet Nam
134	WESTPORTS HOLDINGS BERHAD	Malaysia
135	YINSON HOLDINGS BHD	Malaysia

Source: ACMF Working Group D Secretariat 2019.

Table 3.4:   Top 3 Publicly Listed Companies per Country
(in alphabetical order)

Top 3—INDONESIA
PT BANK CIMB NIAGA TBK.
PT BANK RAKYAT INDONESIA (PERSERO) TBK.
PT BANK TABUNGAN NEGARA (PERSERO) TBK.
Top 3—MALAYSIA
AMMB HOLDINGS BHD
BURSA MALAYSIA BHD
MALAYAN BANKING BHD
Top 3—PHILIPPINES
AYALA LAND, INC.
CHINA BANKING CORPORATION
GLOBE TELECOM, INC.
Top 3—SINGAPORE
SATS LTD
SINGAPORE EXCHANGE LTD
UNITED OVERSEAS BANK LTD
Top 3—THAILAND
BANGCHAK CORPORATION PUBLIC COMPANY LIMITED
PTT PUBLIC COMPANY LIMITED
THAI OIL PUBLIC COMPANY LIMITED
Top 3—VIET NAM
FPT CORPORATION
NOVALAND GROUP
VIET NAM DAIRY PRODUCTS JOINT STOCK COMPANY

Source: ACMF Working Group D Secretariat 2019.

Country Reports and Assessments

INDONESIA

Background of the Corporate Governance Framework

To comprehend how corporate governance is implemented in Indonesia, it is imperative to first understand the legal framework for a limited liability company (PT or Perseroan Terbatas) in Indonesia.

In accordance with Law No. 40 of year 2007 about Limited Liability Companies (Company Law), organs of a company consist of the general meeting of shareholders (GMS), board of commissioners (BOC), and board of directors (BOD).

Functions exercised by each of the company's organs shall comply with the prevailing rules and regulations based on the principle that each organ is independent in carrying out their duties, functions, and responsibilities, which are solely for the benefit of the company.

The GMS facilitates shareholders to make important decisions and has all the authorities that are not delegated to the BOC and BOD. The GMS is the organ of the company that has the authority not given to the BOD or the BOC within limits as stipulated in the Company Law, including to appoint and dismiss members of the BOC and BOD.

The BOC is collectively responsible for overseeing and providing advice to the BOD as well as ensuring the implementation of good corporate governance principles, whereas the BOD is fully responsible for the management of the company for the interests and objectives of the company and represents the company both inside and outside the court in accordance with the company's articles of association.

Based on the applicable legal framework, the two-board system in Indonesia is different from the one-board system applicable in other countries. Consequently, there are differences in implementation, such as the independent director function in a single-board system being represented by the independent commissioner function in Indonesia, as well as the reporting structure of certain functions such as an audit committee and internal audit, without sacrificing the essence of good governance principles.

Evolvement

Indonesia has taken steps toward improving corporate governance. The desire to establish a strong corporate governance environment in the country has included several reforms such as the issuance of the Indonesian Corporate Governance Roadmap, launched in 2014 by the Indonesia Financial Services Authority (OJK)—with the support of the World Bank's International Finance Corporation. This roadmap broadly seeks to achieve the following:

- Strengthened supervisory role of company boards.
- Improved quality of disclosure by companies (increased company transparency).
- Greater protections for shareholders and stakeholders.

Regulations were also enacted as part of the reform and demonstrate the commitment to improving corporate governance.

During 2017–2019, there were issuances of the following regulations by OJK:

- OJK Regulation Number 3/POJK.05/2017 dated 11 January 2017 concerning Good Corporate Governance of Guarantee Institutions.
- OJK Regulation Number 10/POJK.04/2017 dated 14 March 2017 concerning Amendment to OJK Regulation Number 32/POJK.04/2014 concerning The Plan for and The Holding of General Meeting of Shareholders of Publicly Listed Companies.
- OJK Regulation Number 11/POJK.04/2017 dated 14 March 2017 concerning Report on Ownership or Any Change in Ownership of Shares in Publicly Listed Companies.
- OJK Regulation Number 51/POJK.03/2017 dated 27 July 2017 concerning Application of Sustainable Finance for Financial Service Providers, Issuers and Publicly Listed Companies.
- OJK Regulation Number 57/POJK.04/2017 dated 26 September 2017 concerning Implementation of Governance in Securities Companies that Conduct Business Activities as Underwriters and Brokers.
- OJK Regulation Number 59/POJK.03/2017 dated 18 December 2017 concerning Implementation of Good Corporate Governance in Provision of Remunerations for Sharia Commercial Banks and Sharia Business Units.
- OJK Regulation Number 75/POJK.04/2017 dated 22 December 2017 concerning Responsibility of The Board of Directors on Financial Statements.
- OJK Circular Number 4/SEOJK.05/2018 dated 25 January 2018 concerning Reports on Implementation of Good Corporate Governance for Venture Capital Companies.
- OJK Regulation Number 10/POJK.04/2018 dated 1 August 2018 concerning Implementation of Good Corporate Governance for Investment Managers.
- OJK Regulation Number 24/POJK.03/2018 dated 10 December 2018 concerning Implementation of Integrated Good Corporate Governance for Sharia Rural Financing Banks.
- OJK Regulation Number 15/POJK.05/2019 dated 12 June 2019 concerning Pension Fund Governance.
- OJK Regulation Number 43/POJK.05/2019 dated 31 December 2019 concerning Amendments to OJK Regulation Number 73/POJK.05/2016 concerning Good Corporate Governance for Insurance Companies.

During 2018 and 2019, OJK with RSM as the domestic ranking body have held several socializations on the expected governance practice and disclosure for publicly listed companies (PLCs) in Indonesia.

When this report was published, OJK also issued updates to its regulations.

Overall Analysis of Corporate Governance Disclosures

There were 100 PLCs assessed in Indonesia, with the selection based on largest market capitalization as at a certain date. The top 100 Indonesia PLCs represent 15.9% of the total number of Indonesia PLCs and account for 84.3% of the total market capitalization as at 31 March 2019.

On average, Indonesia's corporate governance disclosures have slightly improved as evidenced by the increase in score from 70.59 in 2017 to 70.8 in 2019, showing growth of 0.3%. The highest score increased by 3.9%, from 109.61 to 113.84, which was achieved by PLCs in the finance sector. However, the lowest score decreased by 8.12%, from 40.9 to 37.58, which was experienced by PLCs in the consumer goods sector.

INDONESIA

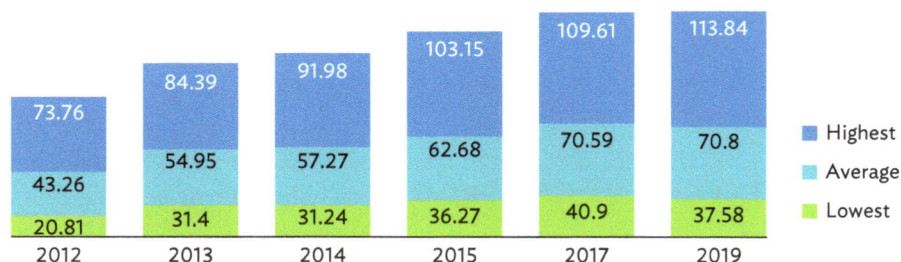

Figure 4.1:   Indonesia Corporate Governance Score, 2012–2019

Source: RSM Indonesia.

The finance sector led with the highest absolute score. However, the highest average score was for the utilities sector. The consumer goods sector had the lowest score, both in absolute and average terms.

Table 4.1:   Indonesia Average Score per Sector

	Average Score	
Sector	2019 (Year End 2018)	2017 (Year End 2016)
Consumer Goods	60.36	60.52
Consumer Services	72.48	63.48
Energy	70.06	60.45
Finance	85.37	85.86
Healthcare	69.46	72.39
Industry	64.47	76.05
Materials	74.48	70.28
Property	64.42	65.92
Technology	68.43	70.84
Telecommunications	71.51	70.80
Utilities	86.13	91.55
	70.80	**70.59**

Source: RSM Indonesia.

Analyzing the average score for 100 PLCs, which fall into 11 sectors, shows four sectors with an increase in the level of disclosures compared to the previous assessment:

- Energy increases to 9.61 or equivalent to 15.90%.
- Consumer services increases by 9.00 or equivalent to 14.18%.
- Material increases to 4.20 or equivalent to 5.98%.
- Telecommunication increases by 0.71 or equivalent to 1%.

On the other hand, the industry sector experiences a significant decrease by 11.58 or equivalent to 15.23%.

The level of disclosures as measured by ASEAN Corporate Governance Scorecard (ACGS) scoring are very much influenced by the changes of PLCs that are included in the assessment for each year, apart from fundamental factors such as tone from the top and motivation to implement ACGS.

Although the highest score increased by 3.9%, unfortunately no representatives of Indonesian PLCs succeeded in entering the Top 20 ASEAN PLCs.

Indonesia's PLCs that attained a score of more than 97.5 increased by 25% from 8 in 2017 to 10 in 2019.

Below are the Indonesian Top 50 PLCs (in alphabetical order).

Table 4.2: Indonesian Top 50 PLCs
(in alphabetical order)

No	Company Name		
1	PT ADIRA DINAMIKA MULTI FINANCE TBK.		
2	PT AKR CORPORINDO TBK.		
3	PT ANEKA TAMBANG TBK.	★	
4	PT ASTRA INTERNATIONAL TBK.		
5	PT BANK CENTRAL ASIA TBK.	★	
6	PT BANK CIMB NIAGA TBK.	★	★
7	PT BANK DANAMON INDONESIA TBK.		
8	PT BANK MANDIRI (PERSERO) TBK.	★	
9	PT BANK MAYBANK INDONESIA TBK.	★	
10	PT BANK MEGA TBK.		
11	PT BANK NEGARA INDONESIA (PERSERO) TBK.		
12	PT BANK OCBC NISP TBK.		
13	PT BANK PAN INDONESIA TBK.		
14	PT BANK PEMBANGUNAN DAERAH JAWA BARAT DAN BANTEN TBK.		
15	PT BANK PERMATA TBK.	★	
16	PT BANK RAKYAT INDONESIA (PERSERO) TBK.	★	★
17	PT BANK TABUNGAN NEGARA (PERSERO) TBK.	★	★
18	PT BANK TABUNGAN PENSIUNAN NASIONAL SYARIAH TBK.		
19	PT BANK TABUNGAN PENSIUNAN NASIONAL TBK.		
20	PT BUKIT ASAM TBK.		
21	PT CHANDRA ASRI PETROCHEMICAL TBK.		
22	PT CIKARANG LISTRINDO TBK.		
23	PT DIAN SWASTATIKA SENTOSA TBK.		
24	PT ELANG MAHKOTA TEKNOLOGI TBK.		
25	PT GARUDA INDONESIA (PERSERO) TBK.		
26	PT GOLDEN ENERGY MINES TBK.		
27	PT H.M. SAMPOERNA TBK.		
28	PT INDO TAMBANGRAYA MEGAH TBK.		
29	PT INDOCEMENT TUNGGAL PRAKARSA TBK.		
30	PT INDOSAT TBK.		

continued on next page

Table 4.2:   Indonesian Top 50 PLCs (*continued*)

No	Company Name	
31	PT JAPFA COMFEED INDONESIA TBK.	
32	PT JASA MARGA (PERSERO) TBK.	★
33	PT KALBE FARMA TBK.	
34	PT KIMIA FARMA (PERSERO) TBK.	
35	PT MATAHARI DEPARTMENT STORE TBK.	
36	PT MITRA KELUARGA KARYASEHAT TBK.	
37	PT MULTI BINTANG INDONESIA TBK.	
38	PT PAKUWON JATI TBK.	
39	PT PERUSAHAAN GAS NEGARA (PERSERO) TBK.	
40	PT PP (PERSERO) TBK.	
41	PT SARANA MENARA NUSANTARA TBK.	
42	PT SEMEN BATURAJA (PERSERO) TBK.	
43	PT TELEKOMUNIKASI INDONESIA (PERSERO) TBK.	
44	PT UNILEVER INDONESIA TBK.	
45	PT UNITED TRACTORS TBK.	
46	PT VALE INDONESIA TBK.	
47	PT WASKITA BETON PRECAST TBK.	
48	PT WASKITA KARYA (PERSERO) TBK.	
49	PT WIJAYA KARYA (PERSERO) TBK.	
50	PT XL AXIATA TBK.	★

Legend:

★ ASEAN Asset Class.

★ Country Top 3.

Source: RSM Indonesia.

Distribution of Scores

The distribution of scores improved compared to the 2017 assessment, predominantly in the number of PLCs that attained a score of more than 97.5, which increased by 25%. In 2017, there were only 8 PLCs, and this increased to 10 in 2019.

Figure 4.2:   Number of PLCs by Sector Within Score Range

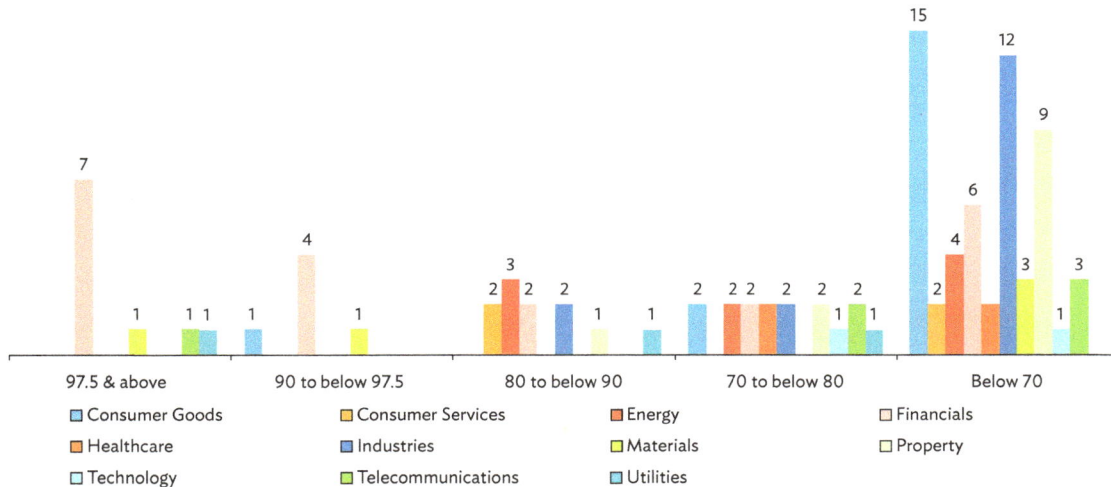

Source: RSM Indonesia.

By Industry Sector

The finance sector led with an absolute highest score and the second highest average score compared to other sectors. Utilities sector showed the highest average score however there were only 3 PLCs included in the 2019 assessment. This might be significantly influenced by the regulation environment for the finance sector, predominantly banking, that are stricter compared to others. In contrast, the consumer goods sector had the lowest score in both absolute and average.

Figure 4.3:   Scoring Distribution by Industry Sector

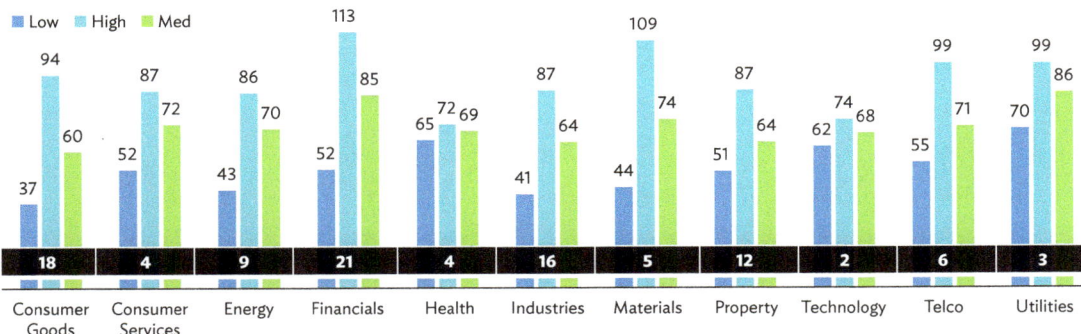

Source: RSM Indonesia.

Market Capitalization

In terms of market capitalization, the assessment showed no correlation between the score and size of PLCs. A larger market cap does not correlate with a higher score in the disclosure assessment.

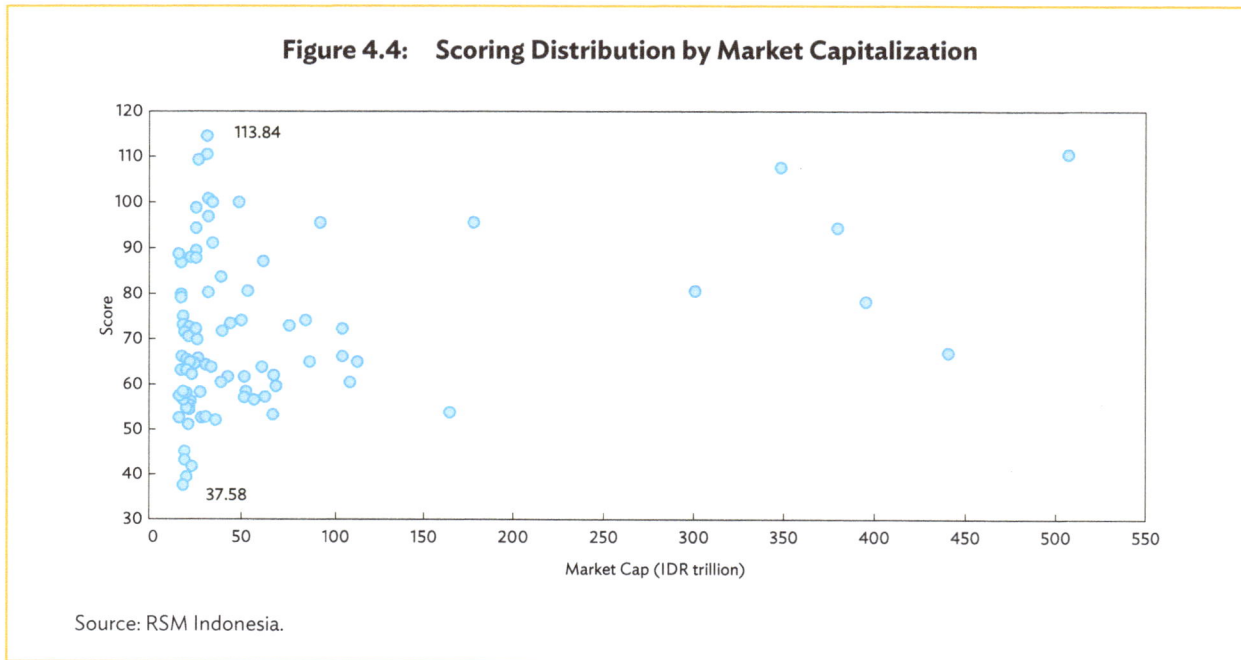

Figure 4.4:   Scoring Distribution by Market Capitalization

Source: RSM Indonesia.

Of the 10 PLCs that scored 97.5 and above, seven have a market cap of below IDR50 trillion. A similar condition also applies for the 6 PLCs that scored 90 to below 97.5, of which 3 have market cap of below IDR50 trillion.

Part A: Rights of Shareholders

All Indonesian PLCs scored best in this part; the adoption rate for all PLCs was above 61.9%, and average adoption rate was 81.3%. The maximum attainable score was 10 and five PLCs fully met all parameters.

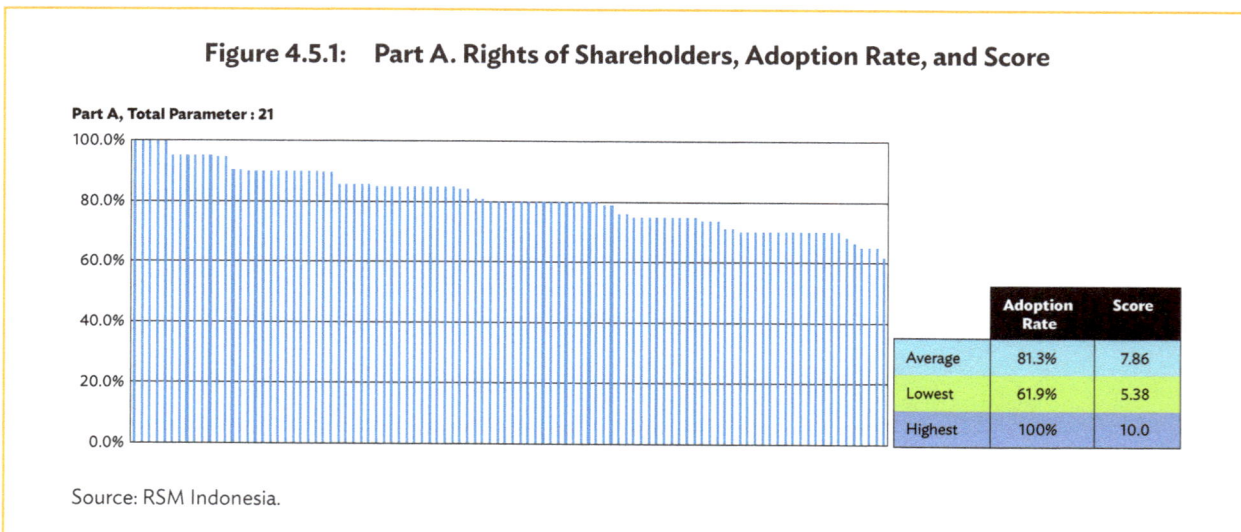

Figure 4.5.1:   Part A. Rights of Shareholders, Adoption Rate, and Score

Part A, Total Parameter : 21

	Adoption Rate	Score
Average	81.3%	7.86
Lowest	61.9%	5.38
Highest	100%	10.0

Source: RSM Indonesia.

Strengths

Key strong points in Part A include the following:

- Shareholders' right to participate in amendments to the company's constitution.
- On the conduct of annual general meetings (AGMs):
    - Notice was provided at least 21 days in advance.
    - Shareholders have the opportunity to place item(s) on the agenda.
    - Shareholders can vote in absentia.
    - Shareholders have the opportunity to approve remuneration or any increases in remuneration for the BOD and BOC.
    - Director/Commissioner elected individually.

Areas for Improvement

The key areas for improvement in Part A relate to the shareholders' right to participate effectively in and vote in general shareholder meetings and information on the rules, including voting procedures that govern general shareholder meetings, which include the following:

- Appointment of an independent party to count and/or validate the votes at the AGM.
- All board members and the chief executive officer (CEO) to attend AGMs.
- Make publicly available by the next working day the result of the votes taken during AGMs/extraordinary general meetings for all resolutions.

Part B: Equitable Treatment of Shareholders

In this part, the average adoption rate is around 64.2%. The maximum attainable score is 15, and 6 PLCs adopted all parameters suggested in this part of the scorecard.

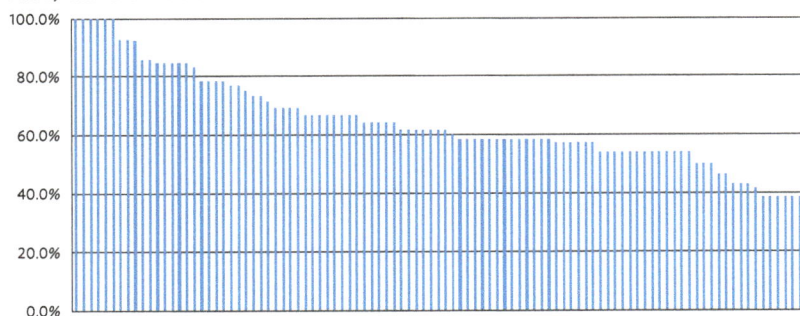

Figure 4.5.2: Part B. Equitable Treatment of Shareholders, Adoption Rate, and Score

Part B, Total Parameter : 15

	Adoption Rate	Score
Average	64.2%	6.57
Lowest	38.5%	4.44
Highest	100%	10.0

Source: RSM Indonesia.

INDONESIA

Strengths

Key strong points in Part B include the following:

- Ordinary or common shares have one vote for one share.
- Policy requiring directors/commissioners to disclose their interest in transactions and any other conflicts of interest.
- Each resolution in the AGM deals with only one item, i.e., there is no bundling of several items into the same resolution.

Areas for Improvement

The key areas for improvement in Part B follow:

- Proxy documents for AGM purposes to be made easily available.
- A policy that requires directors/commissioners to report their dealings in company shares within 3 business days to manage risk of insider trading and abusive self-dealing.
- Policies on loans to directors and commissioners, either forbidding this practice or ensuring that they are being conducted at arm's length and at market rates, to manage the related party transactions by directors and key executives.

Part C: Role of Stakeholders

In this part, the average adoption rate is above 67.5%. The maximum attainable score is 15, and 8 PLCs fully adopted all the parameters.

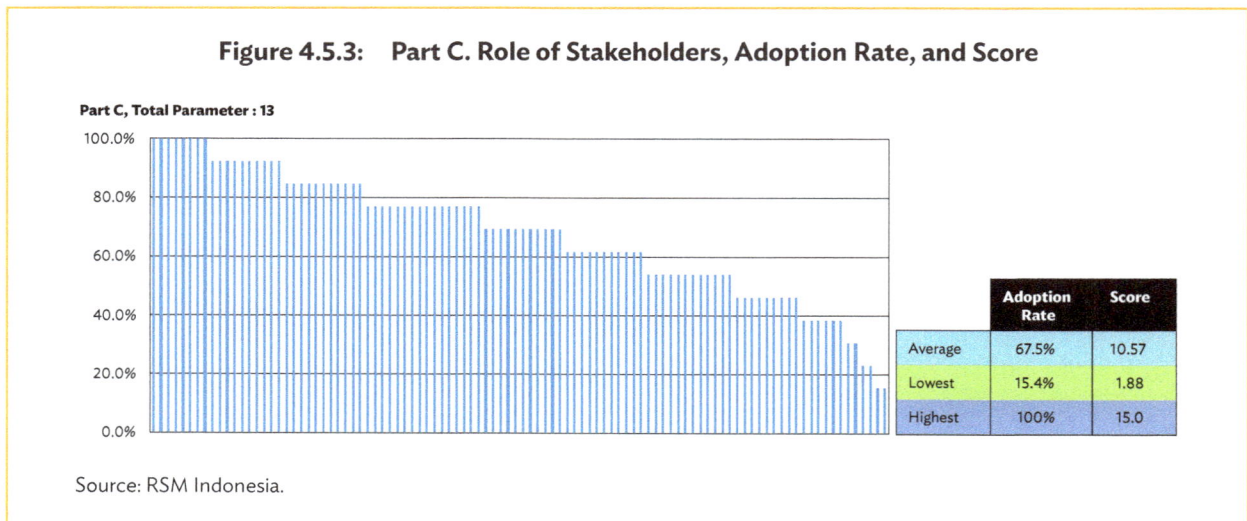

Figure 4.5.3:   Part C. Role of Stakeholders, Adoption Rate, and Score

	Adoption Rate	Score
Average	67.5%	10.57
Lowest	15.4%	1.88
Highest	100%	15.0

Source: RSM Indonesia.

Strengths

Key strong points in Part C include:

*   Efforts to interact with the communities in which the PLC operates.
*   Availability of separate report/section that discusses PLC's efforts on environment/economy and social issues.
*   Contact details that stakeholders can use to voice their concerns and/or complaints for possible violation of their rights.
*   Policies and practices on health, safety, and welfare of the employees.
*   Policies and practices on training and development programs for the employees.

Areas for Improvement

The key areas for improvement in Part C are as follows:

*   Rights of stakeholders that are established by law or through mutual agreements are to be respected. Among the improvements needed, most attention should be given to disclosure of policies and practices that address supplier/contractor selection procedures, and to the disclosure of policies and practices that address how creditors' rights are safeguarded.
*   Mechanisms for employee participation should be permitted to develop. Thus a PLC should have a reward/compensation policy that accounts for the performance of the company beyond short-term financial measures.

Part D: Disclosure and Transparency

In this part, the average adoption rate is around 69.1%. No PLC obtained the maximum attainable score of 25.

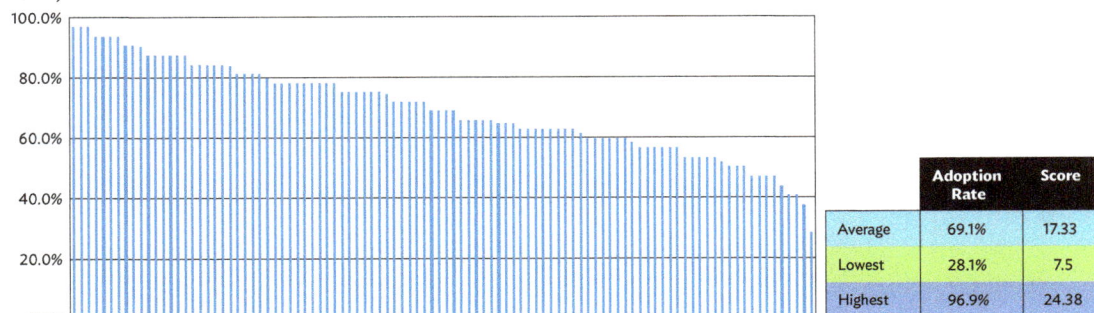

Figure 4.5.4:   **Part D. Disclosure and Transparency, Adoption Rate, and Score**

	Adoption Rate	Score
Average	69.1%	17.33
Lowest	28.1%	7.5
Highest	96.9%	24.38

Source: RSM Indonesia.

Strengths

Key strong points in Part D include:

- Information on shareholdings reveals the identity of beneficial owners holding 5% shareholding or more.
- Disclosure of the direct and indirect shareholdings of major and/or substantial shareholders.
- Disclosure on details of the parent/holding company, subsidiaries, associates, joint ventures, and special purpose enterprises/vehicles.
- Annual report discloses financial performance indicators and biographical details of all directors/commissioners.
- The use of quarterly reporting and website as modes of communication.
- Annual report released within 120 days of the financial year end.
- Has a website disclosing up-to-date financial statements/reports and with a downloadable annual report.

Areas for Improvement

The key areas for improvement in Part D are as follows:

- Disclosure of the direct and indirect shareholdings of senior management.
- Disclosure of total remuneration of each member of the BOD/commissioner in the annual report.
- Has a website disclosing up-to-date articles of association.

Part E: Responsibilities of the Board

In this part, the average adoption rate is around 64.1%. Only one PLC obtained the maximum attainable score of 40.

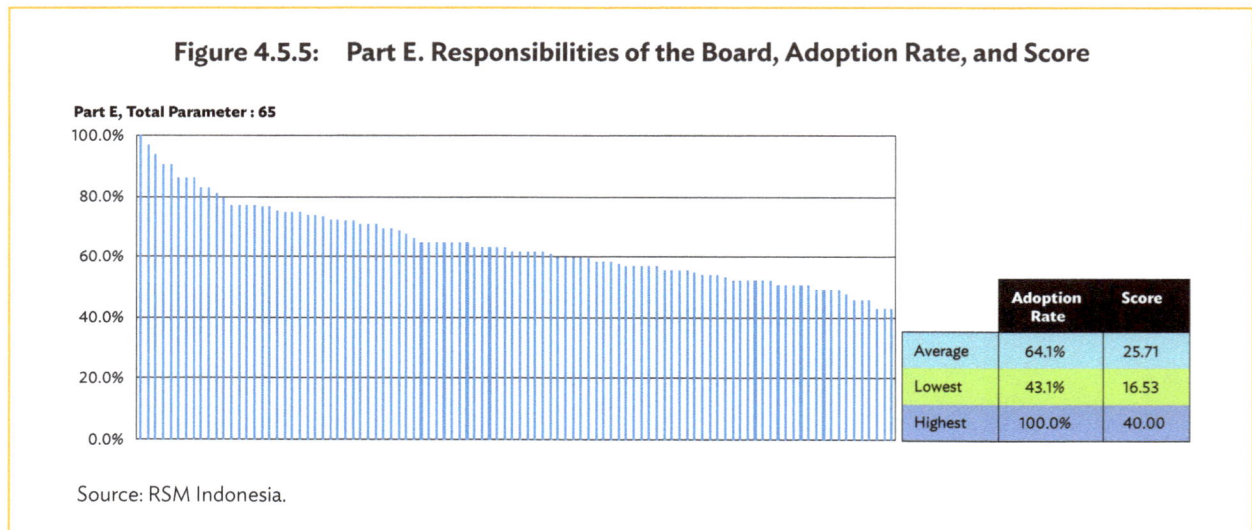

Figure 4.5.5:   Part E. Responsibilities of the Board, Adoption Rate, and Score

Part E, Total Parameter : 65

	Adoption Rate	Score
Average	64.1%	25.71
Lowest	43.1%	16.53
Highest	100.0%	40.00

Source: RSM Indonesia.

Strengths

Key strong points in Part E include the following:

- Disclosure of PLC's corporate governance policy/board charter, audit committee charter, and nomination/ remuneration committee charter.
- Roles and responsibilities of the BOD/BOC are clearly stated, and that each board meet at least six times during the year. In addition, due to the two-board system in Indonesia, different persons assume the roles of chair and CEO.
- Nomination and remuneration committee is chaired by an independent commissioner and comprises a majority of independent members.
- Audit committee is chaired by an independent commissioner, comprised entirely of non-executive and with a majority of independent members with at least one member having accounting qualification or experience. The audit committee's meeting attendance is also disclosed and they meet at least four times during the year.
- There is a separate internal audit function, and the head is clearly identified.
- Disclosure of key risks that PLC is materially exposed to.

Areas for Improvement

The key areas for improvement in Part E are as follows:

- A minimum quorum of at least two-thirds for board decisions.
- Board papers for BOD/commissioners' meetings provided to the board at least 5 business days in advance of the board meeting.
- Existence of measurable standards to align the performance-based remuneration of the executive directors and senior executive with long-term interests of the company, such as claw-back provision and deferred bonuses.

Bonus and Penalty

Level 2 is the bonus and penalty section. Scores from this section are added to the scores in Level 1 to obtain the total score. A positive net score will increase the total score, and a negative net score will result in a reduction. Bonus points are intended to motivate companies to adopt corporate governance practices beyond minimum expected practice for ASEAN PLCs (Level 1), while penalty points are intended to eliminate violations of laws and regulations, inconsistency of stated policies, and other poor corporate governance practices.

Areas for Improvement

The key areas for improvement in this section are as follows:

- Release notice of AGM at least 28 days before the date of the meeting.
- Nominating committee to entirely comprise independent commissioners and parties.
- Disclosure on details of CEO's remuneration.
- Nominating committee undertake the process of identifying the quality of directors aligned with the company's strategic directions.

INDONESIA

- Independent commissioners make up more than 50% of the BOC for a company, with an independent chair.
- Have a separate board-level risk committee.
- Independent commissioners not to receive options, performance shares, or bonuses.

Conclusions and Recommendations

Indonesia's average country score showed growth of 0.3%, from 70.59 in 2017 to 70.80 in 2019. The highest score increased by 3.9%, from 109.61 to 113.84. However, the lowest score decreased by 8.12%, from 40.90 to 37.58.

Indonesia's PLCs that attained a score of more than 97.5 increased by 25% from 8 PLCs in 2017 to 10 in 2019.

The top three significant improvements found in the 2019 assessment are as follows:

- Disclosure of practices to encourage shareholders to engage the company beyond the AGM.
- Disclosure of the policies and practices on health, safety, and welfare of the employees.
- Disclosure of an updated vision and mission statement.

The result of assessment shows that the level of good governance practice and disclosure are more influenced by the tone of the top rather than the size of the company.

In addition, availability of stricter regulations plays a significant role in the adoption of good governance practice, as exhibited by the higher score attained by PLCs in the finance sector, predominantly banking. Thus, applying the same level of expectation to all sectors, not only to the finance sector, could also help in improving corporate governance practice and disclosure in Indonesia.

INDONESIA

MALAYSIA

Corporate Governance Landscape and Developments (2017–2019)

Over the last 3 years, the Malaysian capital market regulators implemented several measures to strengthen the corporate governance framework and advocate the adoption of corporate governance best practices as an integral component of maintaining trust and confidence in the Malaysian capital market.

The Securities Commission Malaysia (SC) announced its 3-year corporate governance strategic priorities in April 2017 to strengthen the corporate governance framework in Malaysia, with five corporate governance strategic priorities being identified for implementation.

An immediate deliverable was the enhanced Malaysian Code on Corporate Governance (MCCG) released in 2017 whereby the code took on a new approach to promote greater internalization of corporate governance culture. The new MCCG dealt with strengthening independence of the board, board diversity, transparency in directors' remuneration, strengthening independence of the audit committee, establishment of a risk management committee, and participation at general meetings. The new MCCG also set a higher expectation on the best practices of the FTSE Bursa Malaysia Top 100 Index companies, and those with a market capitalization of RM2 billion or more. Another new dimension was the introduction of "Step Up" practices to encourage companies to go further in achieving corporate excellence.

Bursa Malaysia as the frontline regulator also played an important role in inculcating a better and stronger corporate governance culture and sustainability practices in the capital market. In April 2018, Bursa Malaysia launched BURSASUSTAIN, a comprehensive online portal designed as a one-stop knowledge and information hub on corporate governance and sustainability. The hub aims to provide a platform for users, such as publicly listed companies (PLCs), investors, and other key stakeholders, with easy access to the latest information on corporate governance and sustainability.

In January 2019, the Malaysian government launched a 5-year National Anti-Corruption Plan (NACP) with the aim of making Malaysia a corruption-free nation by 2023. In line with the goals of the NACP, the SC implemented measures to strengthen the resilience of PLCs and capital market intermediaries against the threat of corruption. Among measures undertaken were the introduction of requirements for PLCs to have robust anti-corruption frameworks in place. Meanwhile, Bursa Malaysia issued a consultation paper in 2019 proposing to introduce various anti-corruption measures for PLCs, among others, requiring boards to establish and maintain policies and procedures on anti-corruption and whistle-blowing, conduct annual reviews of such policies and procedures, and include corruption risk in PLCs' annual risk assessment framework.

The SC published its inaugural edition of the Corporate Governance Monitor 2019 (CG Monitor) in May 2019. The CG Monitor presented the SC's observations in relation to the adoption of the MCCG, quality of disclosures in corporate governance reports of PLCs, and various thematic reviews. The 2019 publication featured thematic reviews on long-serving independent directors, gender diversity on boards and senior management, and chief executive officer (CEO) remuneration of the top 100 listed companies on the Main Market of Bursa Malaysia.

The Minority Shareholders Watch Group (MSWG) as the domestic ranking body for the ASEAN CG Scorecard assessment had conducted engagement sessions with the board and key senior management of PLCs outside of the annual general meeting (AGM) platform. This proactive dialogue approach is a valuable tool to convey our expectations on corporate governance best practices as well as other issues highlighted by minority shareholders. The advocacy programs and engagements on the expectations of the ASEAN CG Scorecard were also successful—many Malaysian PLCs had improved their corporate governance practices, as measured by the 2019 CG Scorecard assessment. For Malaysia, the assessments were carried out not only on the top 100 PLCs according to the market capitalization under the ASEAN project, but were also extended to all other Malaysian PLCs. In total, 866 PLCs were assessed in 2019.

Overall Analysis

The 2019 assessment was undertaken on 100 Malaysian PLCs based on market capitalization as at 31 March 2019. The combined market capitalization of the top 100 PLCs was RM1,443.74 billion, representing 84% of Bursa Malaysia's total market capitalization.

The overall average corporate governance scores have steadily improved since 2012, from 62.29 points in 2012 to 94.31 points in 2019. Over the last 2 years from 2017 to 2019, the overall average corporate governance score for the top 100 Malaysian PLCs increased by 11.90 points (from 82.41 points in 2017 to 94.31 points in 2019), with a maximum score of 129.46 points and a minimum score of 67.45 points compared to 122.58 and 48.82 points in 2017, respectively.

Figure 5.1 shows the overall performance of the top 100 PLCs from 2012 to 2019, excluding 2016 and 2018 because no regional assessments were conducted in these 2 years.

Figure 5.1: Overall CG Score of Top 100 PLCs, 2012–2015, 2017, and 2019

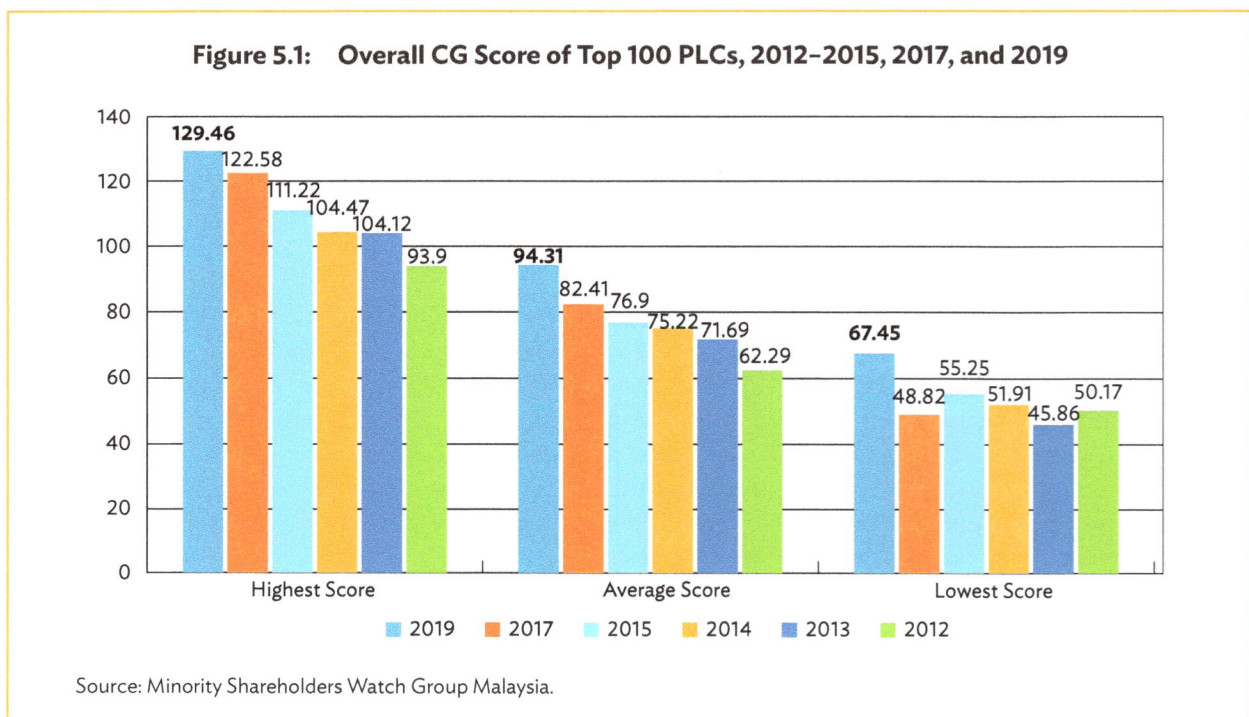

Source: Minority Shareholders Watch Group Malaysia.

Performance by Score Range

Figure 5.2 shows an encouraging trend whereby the number of PLCs that scored above 90 points increased from only 1 in 2012, to 19 in 2015, and leaped to 61 in 2019. Another notable improvement was that the lowest PLC score in 2019 was in the 60–69.9 points band, compared to lowest scores below 50 points in 2012 and 2013.

Figure 5.2:   Overall CG Score of Top 100 PLCs (by Band), 2012–2015, 2017, and 2019

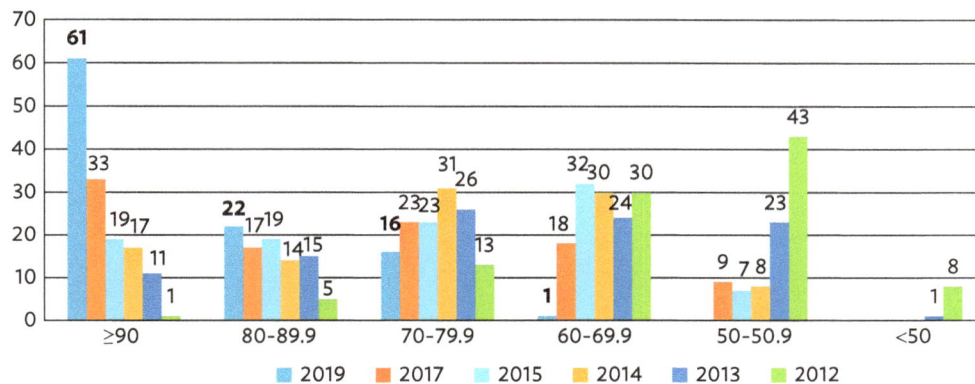

Source: Minority Shareholders Watch Group Malaysia.

Performance by Industry Groups

The top three industry groups in 2019 were telecommunications and media, financial services, and construction sectors (Figure 5.3). Bursa Malaysia had enhanced the sector classification in 2018, to align the exchange's sector classification with internationally recognized standards. The top three industry groups in 2017 (based on the previous sector classification) were finance, industrial products, and trading/service sectors.

Figure 5.3:   Average CG Score of Top 100 PLCs (by Sector)

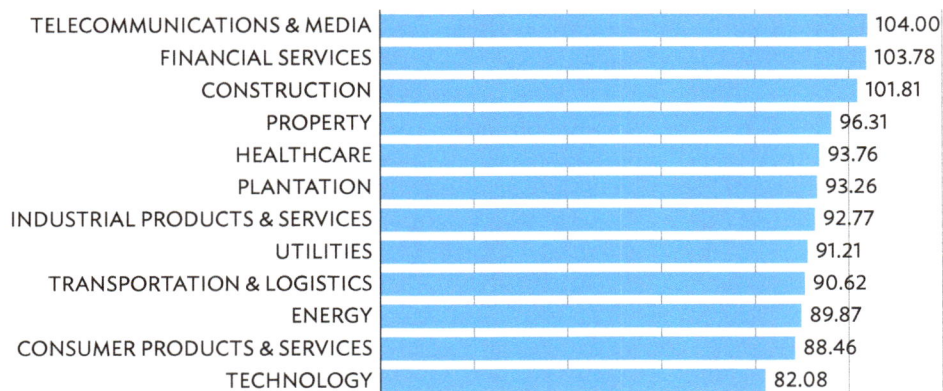

Sector	Average CG Score
TELECOMMUNICATIONS & MEDIA	104.00
FINANCIAL SERVICES	103.78
CONSTRUCTION	101.81
PROPERTY	96.31
HEALTHCARE	93.76
PLANTATION	93.26
INDUSTRIAL PRODUCTS & SERVICES	92.77
UTILITIES	91.21
TRANSPORTATION & LOGISTICS	90.62
ENERGY	89.87
CONSUMER PRODUCTS & SERVICES	88.46
TECHNOLOGY	82.08

Source: Minority Shareholders Watch Group Malaysia.

MALAYSIA

Performance by Components

On average, Malaysian PLCs performed better across all parts in 2019 compared to 2017, with the biggest improvements in Parts C and E. Table 5.1 shows the distribution of average scores for the top 100 PLCs since 2012.

Table 5.1:   Malaysia—Distribution of Average Scores for Top 100 PLCs, 2012–2015, 2017, and 2019

Score (Points)	Year	Part A	Part B	Part C	Part D	Part E
Average Score	2019	8.75	8.94	12.83	19.67	32.14
	2017	8.47	8.92	11.57	18.80	29.83
	2015	6.19	13.03	6.68	18.86	28.86
	2014	5.95	13.60	6.40	18.60	27.96
	2013	5.18	12.81	5.88	17.23	25.19
	2012	5.11	13.38	5.86	16.55	21.54
Highest Score	2019	10.00	10.00	15.00	25.00	39.46
	2017	10.00	10.00	15.00	23.75	39.46
	2015	9.60	15.00	10.00	23.78	37.84
	2014	9.20	15.00	10.00	23.78	37.87
	2013	8.80	15.00	10.00	23.13	35.79
	2012	7.31	15.00	10.00	22.02	33.92
Maximum Possible Score	2017–2019	10.00	10.00	15.00	25.00	40.00
	2012–2015	10.00	15.00	10.00	25.00	40.00

Source: Minority Shareholders Watch Group Malaysia.

Part A: Rights of Shareholders

In 2019, the top 100 PLCs scored an average of 8.75 points out of a maximum of 10.00. This reflected an improvement of 3.3% from 8.47 points in 2017. There were 12 default items for Malaysian PLCs in this category.

All resolutions for Malaysian PLCs were voted via poll as mandated under the listing requirements, with independent scrutineers appointed to validate the votes. All voting results were made publicly available on the Bursa Malaysia website by the following working day, with voting results clearly tabulated for all resolutions tabled at the AGM.

Significant improvement could be seen in the opportunity for shareholders to approve non-executive directors' remuneration whereby, in 2019, all PLCs accorded shareholders the opportunity to approve remuneration (fees, allowances, benefits-in-kind, and other emoluments) or any increase in remuneration for the non-executive directors. The improvement could also be attributed to the requirement of Section 230(1) of the Companies Act 2016, which introduced the requirement for all fees of directors and any benefits payable to directors (including any compensation for loss of employment) of a public company (listed or otherwise) to be approved by the shareholders at a general meeting.

A positive observation is that more companies (86%) published the questions and answers during the AGM proceedings in the AGM minutes. However, this area could be further improved.

The number of PLCs paying their dividends within 30 days from the date of declaration or approval remains one of the key areas for improvement for Malaysian PLCs. Other areas for improvement include providing more detailed minutes of AGMs, which include attendance of board members and the CEO, providing at least 21 days' notice period for extraordinary general meetings (EGMs) and disclosing practices on engagement with shareholders beyond the AGM platform as a means of facilitating the exercise of shareholders' ownership rights. This could be in the form of dialogs with institutional investors.

Figure 5.4:   Malaysia—Strengths and Areas for Improvement in Rights of Shareholders

Strengths

- All resolutions voted via poll voting, and independent scrutineers appointed to validate the votes
- Voting results disclosed showing clearly the approving and dissenting votes for all resolutions tabled at the AGM
- Shareholders had the opportunity to approve non-executive directors' remuneration
- Most companies provided the rationale and explanation for each agenda item
- More companies disclosed the questions and answers during the AGM proceedings in the AGM minutes

Areas for Improvement

- Dividends should be paid in a timely manner
- Publication of the questions and answers during AGM proceedings in the AGM minutes
- Publication of the list of board members' attendance at the AGM, including the CEO (if not a board member)
- Notice of 21 days for EGMs
- Companies to disclose practices to encourage shareholders, including institutional investors, to engage with the companies beyond the AGM

Source: Minority Shareholders Watch Group Malaysia.

Part B: Equitable Treatment of Shareholders

This category examined the equitable treatment of shareholders in the company where 7 of the 15 parameters were default response items. The average score showed a marginal increase to 8.94 points compared to 8.92 points in 2017.

The Malaysian regulatory framework supports equitable treatment of shareholders as evidenced by the one-share-one-vote principle. The majority of PLCs (91%) had one class of shares—ordinary shares. For the remaining PLCs with more than one class of shares, the voting rights of such shares were clearly disclosed in the annual report.

The AGM notices for all companies were published in English. Rules prohibiting insider trading and disclosure of directors' conflict of interest in related party transactions (RPTs) were default response items, as there are laws, rules, or regulations in Malaysia dealing with such items. The majority of PLCs (98%) clearly identified the auditors who were seeking re-appointment in the notice of AGM. Disclosure of directors' profiles of those who were seeking election and/or re-election, and directorships in other listed companies could be further improved.

One of the ways for related parties to expropriate minorities would be through abusive RPTs. Instances include selling assets at below market prices, buying assets at inflated prices from connected persons, and providing financial assistance to related parties at terms not at arm's length or on normal commercial terms. Only 26% of the companies clearly disclosed that RPTs were conducted in such a way to ensure that they were fair and at arm's length. The remaining companies did not provide clear disclosures, for example, companies merely disclosed that their RPTs were conducted on a negotiated basis. Such disclosure lacks transparency and clarity, and would not be deemed as fair and at arm's length.

Figure 5.5:   Malaysia—Strengths and Areas for Improvement in Equitable Treatment of Shareholders

Strengths

- Voting rights attached to shares adequately disclosed
- Notice of AGMs and proxy documents easily available
- Auditors seeking re-appointment clearly identified in AGM resolution
- Adequate rules and policies dealing with insider trading, abusive self-dealing, and RPTs by directors
- Decision on RPTs which required shareholders' approval were made by disinterested shareholders

Areas for Improvement

- Disclosure of the profiles of directors seeking election and/or re-election, particularly on directorships in PLCs
- Clear statement that the RPTs conducted were fair and at arm's length

Source: Minority Shareholders Watch Group Malaysia.

Part C: Role of Stakeholders

This category had 13 items that contributed to 15% of the Level 1 score. There were no default items for Malaysian PLCs under this category. The average score showed a commendable 10.9% increase to 12.83 points from 11.57 points in 2017.

Malaysian PLCs were required under the listing requirements to include sustainability statements in their annual report. The 2019 assessment revealed that all PLCs had a separate section in the annual report that disclosed their efforts on environment, economic, and social issues. Companies made commendable disclosures of their policies and practices that elaborated on their efforts to ensure an environmentally friendly value chain, and the extent of the company's efforts to interact with communities. Policies and practices on safeguarding creditors' rights; employees' health, safety, and welfare; as well as staff training and development programs were also clearly disclosed.

Of the PLCs, 85% had established a whistle-blowing policy that clearly disclosed the procedures for complaints and protection of the whistleblower from retaliation when they reveal illegal or unethical behavior. This could be further enhanced by providing clear contact details on the communication channels through which stakeholders could voice their concerns.

Other important areas for improvement include disclosure of policies and procedures relating to customers' welfare, supplier and/or contractor selection practices, reward or compensation policies for employees, and internal anti-corruption programs. Directors need to take steps to address and put in place policies and procedures to deal with these critical factors in sustainable development.

Moving forward, Malaysian PLCs are encouraged to adopt an internationally recognized reporting framework for sustainability (such as Integrated Reporting and GRI G4 Framework). For the 2019 assessment, 64% of the PLCs covered had adopted such a reporting framework, which is a laudable and positive development.

Figure 5.6:   Malaysia—Strengths and Areas for Improvement in Role of Stakeholders

Strengths

- Sustainability statement disclosed in the annual report
- Good disclosure of policies and practices relating to
  - environment-friendly value chain;
  - interaction with communities;
  - safeguarding creditors' rights;
  - health, safety, and welfare policy for employees; and
  - staff training and development programs.
- Whistle-blowing policy well established, including disclosures on its procedures and implementation

Areas for Improvement

- Lack of disclosure on policies and practices relating to
  - customers' welfare;
  - supplier and/or contractor selection practice;
  - reward or compensation policy for employees; and
  - internal anti-corruption programs and procedures.
- Adoption of an internationally recognized reporting framework for sustainability

Source: Minority Shareholders Watch Group Malaysia.

Part D: Disclosure and Transparency

Part D of the scorecard had 32 items that contributed 25% to the Level 1 score. There were no default items under this section for Malaysian PLCs. This section assessed a company's policies and practices in relation to disclosure and transparency of various aspects.

The average score in terms of disclosure and transparency had increased by 4.6% to 19.67 points from 18.80 points in 2017.

All PLCs disclosed a statement confirming the company's full compliance with MCCG and, in instances where there were non-compliance of certain parameters, the company provided explanations for such departures.

All the assessed companies were transparent in terms of their ownership structure. All companies disclosed the direct and indirect shareholdings of directors, and beneficial owners with more than 5% shareholding, as well as the direct and indirect shareholdings of the substantial shareholders. All PLCs disclosed the total remuneration of each member of the board, a significant improvement from 44% in 2017.

In terms of the quality of the annual reports, all the top 100 PLCs disclosed the financial performance indicators, offering a valuable insight to shareholders and investors on the financial health of the company. More companies also disclosed their corporate objectives and non-financial performance indicators: improvements of 84% (79% in 2017) and 91% (73% in 2017), respectively.

All companies disclosed the audit fees and non-audit fees paid and/or payable to the same audit firm. Most of the companies' non-audit fees did not exceed the audit fees, except for seven companies.

All companies had corporate websites that provided information on their financial statements, annual reports, and notices of AGMs. Minutes of AGMs were uploaded to their websites by 90% of the companies, which was a significant improvement on 67% in 2017. Slightly over half (57%) uploaded the company's constitution on their website.

In terms of key areas for improvement, only 5% (4% in 2017) of the companies disclosed details of trading in company's shares by insiders. While disclosures of directors' trading in company shares can be found in the financial statement, it is uncommon for details of trading by other insiders such as key management to be disclosed in the annual report. Disclosure of dividend policy, currently assessed at 47% (2017: 41%), needs to be further improved. Similarly, disclosure of the direct and indirect shareholdings of senior management was also low at 24%.

Disclosures of RPTs also need to be improved, with only 47% deemed to have adequately disclosed the name, relationship, nature, and value for each material and/or significant RPT.

Figure 5.7:   Malaysia—Strengths and Areas for Improvement in Disclosure and Transparency

Strengths

- Disclosure of the identity of the beneficial owners holding 5% shareholding or more
- Disclosure of the direct and indirect shareholdings of substantial shareholders and directors
- Disclosure of adoption of the practices in the MCCG
- Disclosure of financial performance indicators
- Disclosure of remuneration of individual directors
- Disclosure of audit and non-audit fees
- All PLCs had accessible and informative corporate websites

Areas for Improvement

- Disclosure of direct and indirect shareholdings of senior management
- Disclosure of details of trading in the company's shares by insiders
- Disclosure of name, relationship, nature, and value for each material and/or significant related party transaction
- Disclosure of dividend policy in annual report
- Disclosure of constitution in the corporate website

Source: Minority Shareholders Watch Group Malaysia.

Part E: Responsibilities of the Board

The final section of the scorecard had 65 items that contributed 40% to the Level 1 score. Out of these 65 items, 9 were default items for Malaysian PLCs. In the 2019 assessment, the top 100 PLCs scored an average of 32.14 points compared to 29.83 points in 2017.

All Malaysian PLCs clearly disclosed the roles and responsibilities of the board in the annual report, with 97% clearly disclosing the board charter as well as the types of decisions that required board of directors' approval, which among others cover acquisitions and disposals, share issuance, financial structuring, and risk oversight. Nevertheless, more companies need to clearly disclose their company's vision and mission statement in the annual report.

The number of companies that established a code of ethics improved from 71% in 2017 to 95% in 2019. It is pertinent that a company either has a single code of ethics applicable to all directors and employees or separate codes for directors and employees. Companies were expected to develop a code of ethics according to their specific operations and nature of business, instead of just adopting the pro-forma code of ethics issued by the Companies Commission of Malaysia. Companies should also explain how it implemented and monitored compliance.

All PLCs disclosed that the board took the lead in the review of their annual corporate strategies; 81% disclosed that the board had a process to review, monitor, and oversee the implementation of the corporate strategy.

In relation to board structure, 84% of the companies had different persons assuming the roles of chair and CEO, with 44% of the boards led by an independent chair. The separation of the roles of chair and CEO is important in avoiding concentration of power, increasing accountability, and improving the board's capacity for decision-making independent of management.

Three-quarters of the companies had boards with at least 50% independent directors. However, only 20% adopted a term limit of 9 years or less for their independent directors.

Many PLCs vested their audit committee with the primary responsibility for recommending the appointment/removal of the external auditor and for the appointment/removal of the internal auditor. All the top 100 PLCs had established an internal audit function that provided a crucial line of defense to shareholders, which, when applied well, can be an effective assurance provider in the areas of risk, governance, and control. All PLCs disclosed their internal control procedures and/or risk management systems.

Both nomination and remuneration committees were well established in the top 100 PLCs, where the majority comprised independent directors and were chaired by an independent director. The terms of reference for both committees were also disclosed by many PLCs. The disclosure of meeting attendance details for these committees requires further improvement. Such committees should convene at least two meetings in a year to better fulfill their roles and responsibilities.

All PLCs asserted that their company secretary played a significant role in supporting the board in discharging its responsibilities. In terms of distribution of board papers, this could be further improved, as only 63% disclosed that the board papers were provided to the board at least 5 business days in advance of the board meeting.

Disclosure of remuneration matters, especially those related to policies and/or practices for executive directors and CEOs, as well as disclosure of the fee structure for non-executive directors, need to be further improved. The remuneration policy or practices should also indicate whether the company had any measurable standards that aligned the executive directors' remuneration with the long-term interests of the company, such as inclusion of claw-back provision and deferred bonuses.

MALAYSIA

Another area for improvement was in relation to disclosures related to succession planning of the CEO and key management, as only 34% made such disclosures. It is also very important for companies to disclose whether an annual performance assessment was conducted for the CEO—only 42% indicated that such assessment was conducted.

Good corporate governance practice recommends that the board should undertake a formal and rigorous annual evaluation of its own performance and that of its committees as well as individual directors. The assessment this year reflected that a fair number made such assessments, nevertheless there was a lack of disclosure in terms of the process and criteria used for assessment of the board, board committees, and individual directors.

Figure 5.8:   Malaysia—Strengths and Areas for Improvement in Responsibilities of the Board

Strengths

- Disclosure of board charter and roles and responsibilities of the board
- Disclosure of the types of decisions requiring board approval
- Disclosure of board's role in reviewing their annual corporate strategies
- Audit committee has the primary responsibility for recommendation on the appointment and removal of the external auditor and the appointment and removal of the internal auditor
- Disclosure of the internal control procedures and/or risk management systems
- Disclosure of remuneration of individual directors
- Establishment of nomination and remuneration committees

Areas for Improvement

- Board composition to comprise at least 50% independent directors
- Adoption of 9-year term limit for independent directors
- Disclosure of the remuneration policies and/or practices for executive directors and CEOs, as well as disclosure of the fee structure for non-executive directors
- Disclosure of measurable standards which aligned the executive directors' remuneration with the long-term interests of the company
- Disclosure of succession planning of the CEO and key management
- Disclosure of annual performance assessment for CEO
- Disclosure of the process and criteria used for board, board committees, and individual directors' assessments

Source: Minority Shareholders Watch Group Malaysia.

Bonus and Penalty

Malaysian PLCs continue to show improvement when it comes to adopting good corporate governance practices that go beyond items in Level 1 (Figure 5.9). The average overall bonus increased to 13.83 points in 2019 compared to 7.90 points in 2017.

A notable improvement was the number of companies which adopted an internationally recognized reporting framework on sustainability, which increased from 28 companies in 2017 to 64 in 2019. The number of companies with at least one female independent director also increased from 48% in 2017 to 86% in 2019. More companies (64%) had also described their governance process around information technology (IT) issues including disruption, cyber security, and disaster recovery to ensure all key risks were identified. The majority of companies (96%) had released their notice of AGM at least 28 days before the meeting. Companies could improve further by releasing annual audited reports within 60 days from the financial year end and disclosing policy and measurable objectives in implementing board diversity and reporting on its progress.

Companies largely received penalty points for having independent directors who had served the board for more than 9 years. Also, in some instances, the chair of the board was also the CEO of the company in the last 3 years.

As mentioned earlier, PLCs need to disclose the list of board members' attendance at the AGM, including the CEO. The chair, CEO, and audit committee chair attendance at the most recent AGM could not be determined based on the AGM minutes.

There were two companies that received penalty points due to independent directors being granted share options. This practice is generally discouraged and thus was not adopted by majority of the top 100 PLCs.

Figure 5.9: Malaysia—Strengths and Areas for Improvement in Bonus and Penalty Sections

Strengths

- Longer notice period for the AGM (at least 28 days)
- More companies with at least one female independent director on the board
- More companies adopted an internationally recognized reporting framework on sustainability
- Companies disclosed the governance process around IT issues including disruption, cyber security, and disaster recovery

Areas for Improvement

- Companies to release the annual audited report within 60 days of the financial year end
- Companies to adopt a tenure limit of 9 years for independent directors
- Companies to disclose the policies and measurable objectives in implementing board diversity and report on their progress

Source: Minority Shareholders Watch Group Malaysia.

Conclusions and Recommendations

The Malaysian corporate governance framework has been further strengthened with the new MCCG and amendments to the listing requirements, which empower shareholders with better quality information in the annual reports of companies to enable them to make informed investment decisions. The launch of the sustainability framework that mandated sustainability statement on the management of material economic, environmental, and social risks and opportunities created momentum for Malaysian PLCs to seriously embed sustainability principles in their business.

It is heartening to note that despite the overall stricter criteria, with greater emphasis on disclosure of actual practices and inclusion of emerging corporate governance developments in the assessment, the top 100 Malaysian PLCs improved their scores in the 2019 assessment. This is evidenced by the increase in the overall average score of 94.31 points compared to 82.41 in 2017 for the top 100 PLCs, and the increase in the average score to 104.79 points for the top 50 PLCs compared to 95.84 in 2017.

The initiatives taken by MSWG to continue with its approach to engage with the board and key management of PLCs outside the AGM platform also resulted in a greater understanding among PLCs on the importance of internalizing good corporate governance culture in the organization. This, in turn, resulted in more transparent and enhanced disclosures in the annual reports as well as in a willingness to adopt internationally recognized best practices.

However, there are still gaps that need to be addressed, as identified in the analysis of the respective sections. Some key are as follows:

- Publication of AGM minutes should also include the board members' and CEO's attendance, and questions and answers raised at the general meetings. These should be published in a timely manner.
- Disclosure of dividend policy and payment of dividends in a timely manner.
- Clear disclosure on RPTs in the annual report, and that they were fair and conducted at arm's length.
- Disclosure of environmental, social, and governance policies and practices, especially those linking to companies' sustainability and strategy.
- Disclosure on direct and indirect shareholdings of senior management.
- Adoption of a 9-year tenure limit for independent directors.
- Disclosure of board's succession planning process for CEO and key management.
- Disclosure of the remuneration policies and/or practices for executive directors and CEOs, as well as disclosure of the fee structure for non-executive directors.
- Disclosure of measurable standards that align the executive directors' remuneration with the long-term interests of the company.
- Disclosure of a board diversity policy and measurable objectives in implementing board diversity and report on its progress.
- Adoption of an internationally recognized reporting framework on sustainability.

As testimony to the combined efforts by regulators, MSWG, and PLCs in the corporate governance ecosystem, seven Malaysian PLCs were listed in the ASEAN Top 20 PLCs and 37 PLCs received awards for ASEAN Asset Class. These achievements were indeed significant, as companies continue to push themselves forward, not just in the region, but also at the global level. Moving forward, Malaysian PLCs need to keep the momentum going to ensure solid and sound corporate governance remains at the heart of the company to attract investments and maintain investors' confidence in these challenging times.

MALAYSIA

Table 5.2:   Malaysia—Top 50 PLCs in 2019
(in alphabetical order)

No.	Company	No.	Company
1	AIRASIA GROUP BHD	26	MALAYSIAN RESOURCES CORPORATION BHD
2	ALLIANCE BANK MALAYSIA BHD	27	MAXIS BHD
3	ALLIANZ MALAYSIA BHD	28	MISC BHD
4	AMMB HOLDINGS BHD	29	PETRONAS CHEMICALS GROUP BHD
5	ASTRO MALAYSIA HOLDINGS BHD	30	PETRONAS DAGANGAN BHD
6	AXIATA GROUP BHD	31	PETRONAS GAS BHD
7	BIMB HOLDINGS BHD	32	PUBLIC BANK BHD
8	BRITISH AMERICAN TOBACCO (M) BHD	33	RHB BANK BHD
9	BURSA MALAYSIA BHD	34	SIME DARBY BHD
10	CAHYA MATA SARAWAK BHD	35	SIME DARBY PLANTATION BHD
11	CIMB GROUP HOLDINGS BHD	36	SIME DARBY PROPERTY BHD
12	DIGI.COM BHD	37	S P SETIA BHD
13	FRASER & NEAVE HOLDINGS BHD	38	SUNWAY BHD
14	GENTING PLANTATIONS BHD	39	SUNWAY CONSTRUCTION GROUP BHD
15	HONG LEONG BANK BHD	40	SYARIKAT TAKAFUL MALAYSIA BHD
16	IHH HEALTHCARE BHD	41	TELEKOM MALAYSIA BHD
17	IJM CORPORATION BHD	42	TENAGA NASIONAL BHD
18	IOI CORPORATION BHD	43	TIME DOTCOM BHD
19	IOI PROPERTIES GROUP BHD	44	TOP GLOVE CORPORATION BHD
20	KLCC PROPERTY HOLDINGS BHD	45	UEM EDGENTA BHD
21	KPJ HEALTHCARE BHD	46	UEM SUNRISE BHD
22	LPI CAPITAL BHD	47	UMW HOLDINGS BHD
23	MALAYAN BANKING BHD	48	VELESTO ENERGY BHD
24	MALAYSIA AIRPORTS HOLDINGS BHD	49	WESTPORTS HOLDINGS BHD
25	MALAYSIA BUILDING SOCIETY BHD	50	YINSON HOLDINGS BHD

Source: Minority Shareholders Watch Group Malaysia.

MALAYSIA

PHILIPPINES

Background of the Corporate Governance Framework

The Philippines officially launched its participation in the ASEAN Corporate Governance Scorecard on 11 September 2012. The Securities and Exchange Commission (SEC) has been working on improving corporate governance practices in the Philippines since the adoption of the scorecard. In 2013, the SEC, along with the Institute of Corporate Directors (ICD), launched an information campaign to familiarize PLCs, other government regulators, and investors with the objectives and mechanics of the scorecard. The SEC required all PLCs to issue an Annual Corporate Governance Report (ACGR), which is intended to consolidate all the governance policies and procedures of each PLC into one report for ease of reference. The SEC further required that all PLCs post their ACGR on their corporate websites. In December 2013, the SEC directed all key officers and members of the board of PLCs to attend a training program on corporate governance at least once a year.

The SEC has recognized the need to update the primary codes that comprised the corporate governance framework in the Philippines. By the first half of 2014, the SEC had amended the Code of Corporate Governance to include "other stakeholders" in companies' responsibilities. To improve the quality of PLCs' websites, the SEC recommended a template for PLCs to follow in organizing disclosures made online. The PLCs were also directed to post the minutes of all general or special meetings within 5 days of the actual date of the meeting.

In 2015, the SEC published the Philippine Corporate Governance Blueprint to serve as a 5-year roadmap for building a strong corporate governance framework. The blueprint was developed through a process that combined using the OECD principles as a reference point for international best practice and through consultation with local PLCs, governance advocates, academe, and corporate governance stakeholders. In line with globally accepted regulatory principles, the guidelines contemplated under the blueprint would be geared not only toward compliance, but also toward enabling companies to deliver performance that contributes to the country's economic and social progress. In this regard, certain identified strategic priorities have been pursued.

In November 2016, the SEC released the Code of Corporate Governance for PLCs, which was designed to raise the corporate governance standards of Philippine corporations to a level at par with its regional and global counterparts. This code was developed using as key reference the Principles of Corporate Governance of the OECD and the ASEAN Corporate Governance Scorecard (ACGS) of the ASEAN Capital Market Forum (ACMF). Accordingly, the PLCs were required to each submit a new manual on corporate governance. The code applies the "comply or explain" approach which combines voluntary compliance with mandatory disclosure. Each company covered by the code must state in its ACGR whether it is compliant with the code's regulatory provisions, identify any areas of non-compliance, and explain the reasons for non-compliance.

Also in 2016, a bill was filed in Congress for the revision of the Corporation Code of the Philippines, which was enacted in May 1980. Although most of the provisions of this law were considered good, it had provisions that many consider antiquated and no longer compatible with current developments.

The SEC issued the Integrated Annual Corporate Governance Report (I-ACGR) in 2017, wherein the corporate governance recommendations of the SEC under the Code of Corporate Governance and the Philippine Stock Exchange (PSE) were harmonized. It must be submitted to the SEC and filed in the company's website on an annual basis. It should also be signed by the company's chair of the board, chief executive officer or president, all independent directors, compliance officer, and corporate secretary.

The Republic Act No. 11232, Revised Corporation Code of the Philippines (RCCP) was implemented on 23 February 2019. It amended the old corporation code and promoted significant changes in the legal framework in the operation of private corporations in the Philippines. It is intended to improve ease of doing business in the country. It simplifies corporate registration, strengthens corporate governance, and amends some existing regulations.

Being the Philippines' domestic ranking body, the ICD facilitated the scoring of all PLCs. The assessment involved selecting and validating the Top 100 PLCs, based on market capitalization, and submitting their scores to the ACMF.

Overall Analysis

The 2019 ACGS assessment was done on each of the top 100 Philippine PLCs as selected based on market capitalization as of 31 March 2019. Given below are the respective numbers of assessed companies belonging to the seven sectors used by the PSE to classify listed companies.

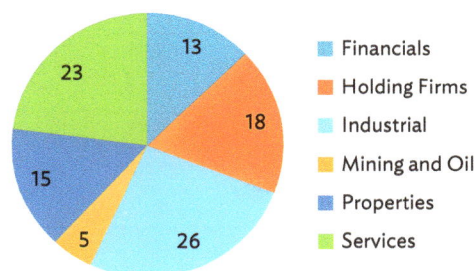

Figure 6.1:   Number of Philippine PLCs for Each Sector

Source: Institute of Corporate Directors Philippines.

Since the launch of the scorecard in the Philippines, the companies have gradually adopted the recommended best corporate governance practices. They started to improve their disclosures and adhere to the corporate governance-related regulations implemented. In 2015, the OECD released its revised Principles of Corporate Governance, which were subsequently endorsed by the G20. In light of this development, the ACMF initiated a review of the ACGS to align it with recent developments and emerging practices. The review was concluded in May 2017 and the resulting revised ACGS was used in the 2017 assessment. This revised version of the ACGS was considered to have raised the bar in the assessment of PLCs. It adopted more stringent criteria for some existing items in the scorecard and incorporated new recommended practices. Thus, the average score of the Top 100 Philippine PLCs by market capitalization dropped to 67.61 points in 2017 from 73.09 points in 2015. Considering this, the companies adjusted again to the changes in the scorecard. This resulted in a total average score of 77.24 points in 2019, an increase of 9.63 points from the last regional assessment in 2017. The improvements in the total average scores across the years are shown in the chart below:

Figure 6.2:   Philippine Top 100 PLCs According to Market Capitalization Total Average Score

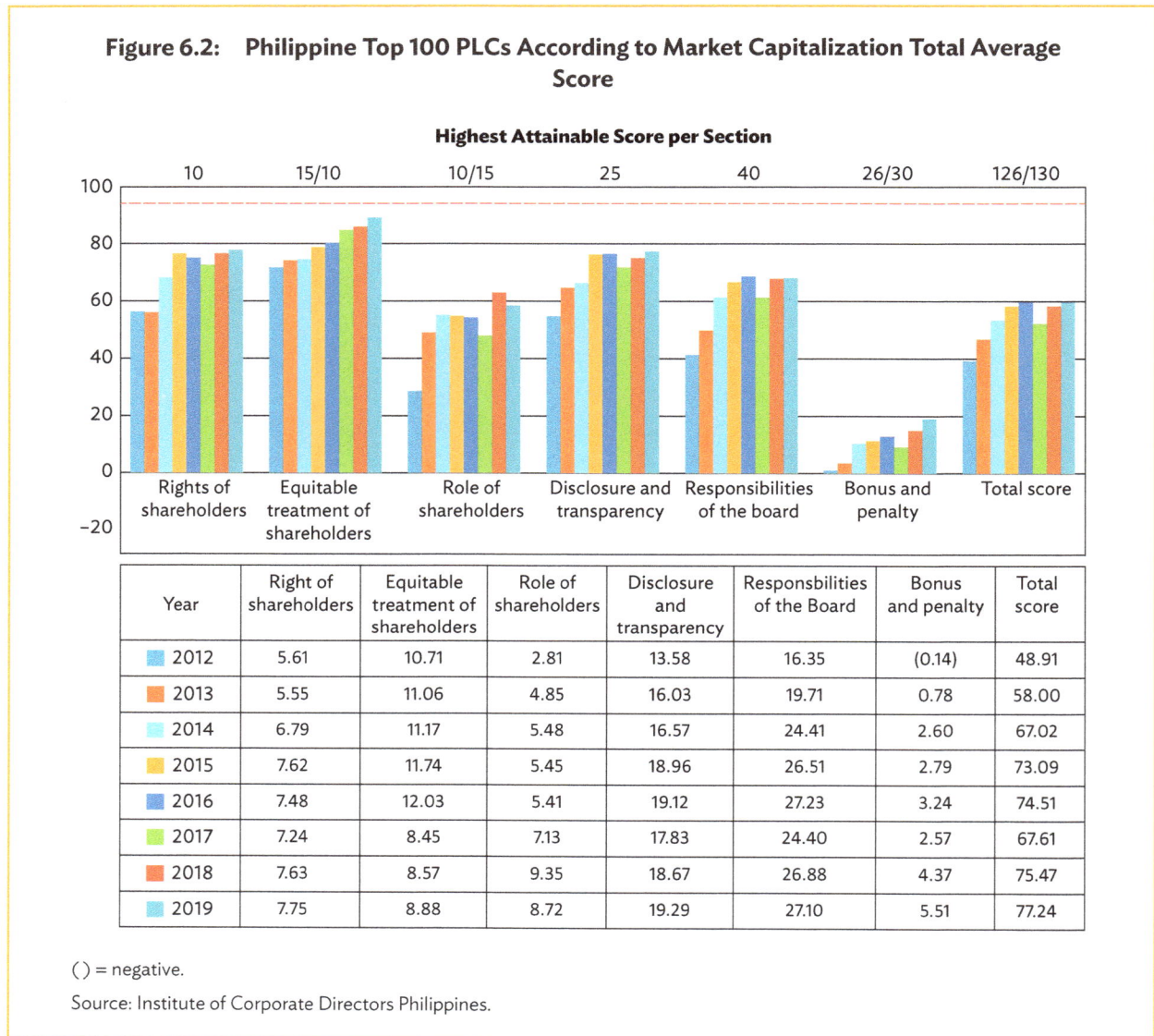

Highest Attainable Score per Section

Year	Right of shareholders	Equitable treatment of shareholders	Role of shareholders	Disclosure and transparency	Responsbilities of the Board	Bonus and penalty	Total score
2012	5.61	10.71	2.81	13.58	16.35	(0.14)	48.91
2013	5.55	11.06	4.85	16.03	19.71	0.78	58.00
2014	6.79	11.17	5.48	16.57	24.41	2.60	67.02
2015	7.62	11.74	5.45	18.96	26.51	2.79	73.09
2016	7.48	12.03	5.41	19.12	27.23	3.24	74.51
2017	7.24	8.45	7.13	17.83	24.40	2.57	67.61
2018	7.63	8.57	9.35	18.67	26.88	4.37	75.47
2019	7.75	8.88	8.72	19.29	27.10	5.51	77.24

( ) = negative.

Source: Institute of Corporate Directors Philippines.

Clearly, improvements are still needed in corporate governance practices in several areas. Special attention should be given to the role of stakeholders (average 8.72 points in 2019 out of 15 possible maximum points) and responsibilities of the board (27.10 points in 2019 out of 40 possible maximum points).

The score distribution chart shows that some companies achieved better performance despite the tough requirements under the ACGS. However, more companies need to step up and adopt the recommended corporate governance practices to improve their ACGS performance.

Figure 6.3:   Philippine Top 100 PLCs According to Market Capitalization Score Distribution

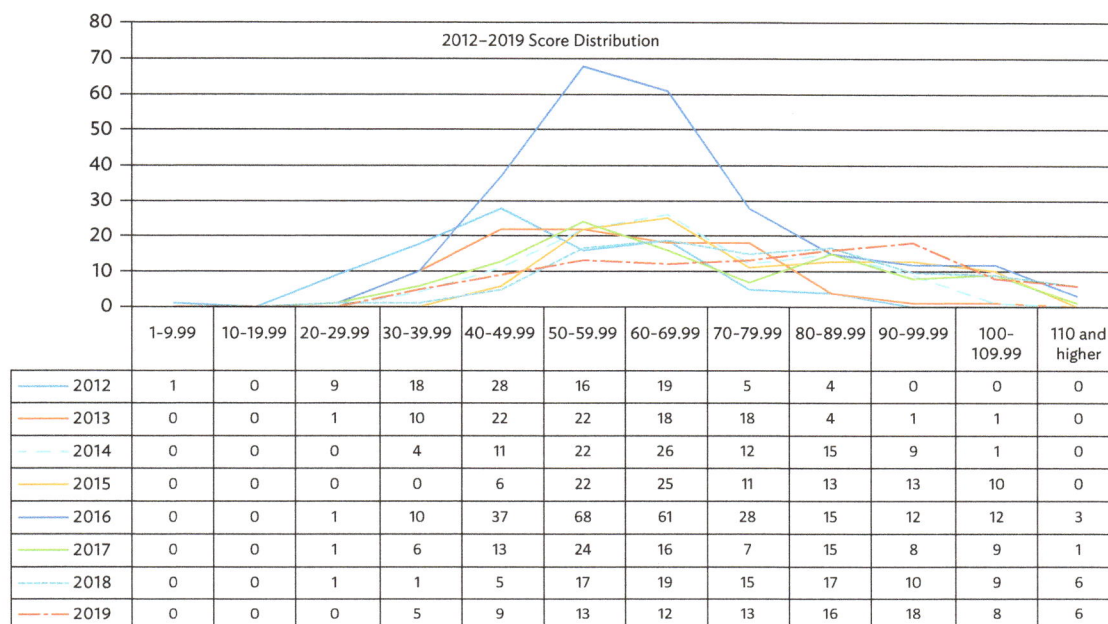

	1-9.99	10-19.99	20-29.99	30-39.99	40-49.99	50-59.99	60-69.99	70-79.99	80-89.99	90-99.99	100-109.99	110 and higher
2012	1	0	9	18	28	16	19	5	4	0	0	0
2013	0	0	1	10	22	22	18	18	4	1	1	0
2014	0	0	0	4	11	22	26	12	15	9	1	0
2015	0	0	0	0	6	22	25	11	13	13	10	0
2016	0	0	1	10	37	68	61	28	15	12	12	3
2017	0	0	1	6	13	24	16	7	15	8	9	1
2018	0	0	1	1	5	17	19	15	17	10	9	6
2019	0	0	0	5	9	13	12	13	16	18	8	6

Source: Institute of Corporate Directors Philippines.

Part A: Rights of Shareholders

The rights of shareholders to participate in decisions concerning fundamental corporate changes are embedded in the 2019 RCCP. Under the RCCP, companies allow their shareholders to elect directors individually. The PLCs' information statements which also serve as the companies' notice of the annual shareholders meeting (ASM) were released 21 days before the ASM. They were also made available on the PSE's website. The quality of the notice of ASM improved over the years as most companies provided explanation of agenda items that require shareholders' approval.

The assessment also found that only a few companies were voting by poll during the ASM. Philippine PLCs have yet to implement activities to engage shareholders including institutional shareholders beyond just attending the ASM.

Strengths

- Notices to ASM were released in a timely manner, i.e., within 21 days before the meeting.
- Voting procedures were disclosed.
- Explanations for agenda items requiring shareholders' approval were provided.

Areas for Improvement

- Companies should engage with shareholders beyond just encouraging them to attend the ASM.
- All board members should attend the ASM.
- Companies should practice voting by poll during the ASM.

Part B: Equitable Treatment of Shareholders

The corporate governance framework should ensure the equitable treatment of all shareholders, including minority and foreign shareholders. To ensure this equitable treatment, directors are required to abstain from participating in discussions when they are conflicted. The RCCP also prohibits any directors, officers, or employees benefiting from knowledge not available to the public. Companies observe the principle of "one common share one vote."

Over the years, disclosures on related party transactions (RPTs) have improved. Many PLCs are already disclosing their policies on RPTs. For some PLCs, a committee mandated to review material or significant RPTs, preferably with no executive directors as members, is still to be established. Names and relationships of parties to material RPTs were disclosed. However, some PLCs did not declare that their RPTs were conducted on an arm's length basis or in normal commercial terms.

Many companies have already required directors and officers to report their dealing in company shares within 3 business days to align with the best practice recommended by the ACGS.

Strengths

- Auditors being appointed/re-appointed during the ASM were identified.
- Most companies' proxy documents were available.
- There is a policy requiring directors to report within 3 business days when they deal with company shares.

Areas for Improvement

- Material or significant RPTs should be reviewed by a committee of independent directors.
- The profile of candidates to the board should include the information recommended by the ACGS.
- RPTs should be conducted in a fair manner and at an arm's length basis or in normal commercial terms.

Part C: Role of Stakeholders in Corporate Governance

This category was where Philippine PLCs received the lowest score. The assessment found that having a separate corporate social responsibility (CSR) section remained a strength of Philippine PLCs. However, the information disclosed in the CSR section of PLCs was not being qualified by the assessment, which was reflected in the assessment of other items under this category. The companies' I-ACGRs were found to be very useful in searching for their policies and activities relating to other stakeholders. However, some PLCs should still review and strengthen their policies and implement activities relating to other stakeholders, including their employees. The PLCs should also provide more specific contact details for other stakeholders to use in raising possible violations of their rights, more than the general contact details usually found on the companies' websites. In addition, PLCs should consider adopting the practice of having a reward policy for employees that accounts for the company's performance beyond short-term financial measures.

Strengths

- Most companies had a separate CSR section in their annual report or on their website.
- Most companies disclosed a whistle-blowing policy that included a provision ensuring the protection of the reporting party from retaliation.

Areas for Improvement

- Performance enhancing mechanisms like employee stock ownership plans should be adopted.
- Contact details of company personnel to whom stakeholders can voice their complaints or concerns should be provided.
- Policies and activities relating to suppliers and creditors should be reviewed and strengthened.

Part D: Disclosure and Transparency

Disclosure is one of two major demands of modern corporate governance. There is a presumption in corporate governance that fuller and more transparent disclosure is a major effective deterrent against corporate governance malpractices. The chapter on disclosure identifies the items that PLCs must disclose to the public to better secure observance of good corporate governance practices. When submission of the I-ACGR has been implemented, it helps the PLCs organize the information, making it easier for stakeholders to access the latest information.

Disclosure of matters on remuneration remain one of the main challenges for Philippine PLCs under this category. The assessment found that it was not clear if most PLCs had conducted analyst and media briefings. Disclosures also did not show the summary of trading of directors and officers of the company on company shares.

Strengths

- Annual reports and audited financial statements were disclosed in a timely manner.
- Direct and indirect shareholdings of substantial shareholders, directors, and officers were disclosed.

Areas for Improvement

- Disclosures on remuneration policies and practices should be improved.
- Annual reports can be improved by including corporate objectives, non-financial performance indicators, and dividend policy.
- Disclosure of transactions by directors and officers on company shares should be made easily accessible.
- Some companies' minutes of the ASM and materials for analyst and media briefings are not available.

Part E: Responsibilities of the Board

The second major demand of modern corporate governance is for the board of directors to step up to the plate and actively take on the role—the duties and responsibilities—that the laws, rules, and regulations vested upon them. The board has the original task, which carries with it the fiduciary duty, of supervising the management of the affairs of the PLC. The first concern that has to be fully addressed is the formulation of a corporate governance policy and within it the definition of board responsibilities.

Many Philippine PLCs are consistently improving their policies and procedures to become more efficient and effective. New recommendations of the new version of ACGS are among those practices they are adopting. They have considered these recommendations in drafting their new Manual on Corporate Governance in compliance with the CG Code for PLCs. The new I-ACGR has improved the disclosures of corporate governance policies and practices of the PLCs. However, there are items that remain a challenge for Philippine PLCs such as increasing the number of independent directors on the board and some protocols recommended by the ACGS. Some of these protocols are the 9-year term limit for independent directors from the date of first appointment, five board seats limit for directors, and non-executive directors meeting separately without the presence of any executives.

Strengths

- Board committees were established to support the board in the effective performance of its functions. Their charters were disclosed.
- Most boards were supported by a corporate secretary with a legal background.
- Criteria and processes in appointing new directors were disclosed.
- Internal audit functions were in place.
- Director development activities such as onboarding programs and continuing professional development were implemented.

Areas for Improvement

- The board should lead the annual review of corporate strategy. This should be articulated in the company's report including the process the board undertakes to accomplish the recommendation.
- Multiple directorships should be limited to five PLCs.
- Board committees should comprise a majority of independent directors.
- Non-executive directors should meet at least once a year without the presence of executive directors.
- Companies should establish measurable standards to align the performance-based remuneration of the executive directors and senior executives with long-term interests of the company.
- Annual performance appraisal of the board, individual directors, and board committees should be conducted. This should include the process and criteria for conducting these assessments.

Bonus and Penalty

Many PLCs released their information statements at least 28 days before the ASM. Pursuant to Section 20 of the Securities Regulation Code, the information statement was used to notify shareholders of any matter that needs to be acted upon during the ASM or other meeting of the shareholders. The results from this year's assessment also indicated that more PLCs had created a separate board-level risk committee. It was also observed that most Philippine PLCs do not meet the recommended practice on the number of independent board members. Some companies even had board members serving as independent directors for more than 9 years. Some companies had board members serving more than five boards of listed companies.

PHILIPPINES

Strengths

- Most companies released their notice of ASM with explanatory circulars 1 month before the meeting.
- Many companies had established a separate board-level risk committee.

Areas for Improvement

- Some independent directors had been serving the company for more than 9 years from the date of first appointment.
- There were directors serving on boards of more than 5 PLCs.

Conclusions and Recommendations

It has always been a challenge for Philippine PLCs to adhere to the best corporate governance practices. The revision of the ACGS in 2017 resulted in a more stringent scorecard. Two years after its implementation, many PLCs did their best to meet the new expectations under the revised ACGS. It should be noted that 71 PLCs achieved a better corporate governance performance in 2019. There were also 19 Philippine PLCs included in the ASEAN Top PLCs based on ACGS performance.

Nevertheless, improvements are needed in corporate governance practices in several areas. Special attention should be given, in particular, to the role of stakeholders. These remain a challenge in how to make most companies adopt these practices, for it has been observed that most of the improvements are concentrated among the larger companies.

The launching of the Code of Corporate Governance for PLCs in 2016 and the RCCP in 2019 were welcome developments. These were progressions toward a better corporate governance regime. For this, the SEC is commended. These codes raised the standards for corporate governance performance given that the guidelines were referenced to the Principles of Corporate Governance of the G20/OECD and criteria of the ACGS. This will help make the corporate governance practices of Philippine PLCs at par with their regional and global counterparts. The use of the "comply or explain" approach in enforcing the code would also provide PLCs the leeway to highlight the specific situations of their sectors or businesses.

For a smooth transition in implementing the code, the SEC issued a memorandum circular that clarifies the submission of the 2016 ACGR. To further improve the disclosures of the PLCs, the SEC released an I-ACGR that will be used as a tool to disclose PLCs' compliance or non-compliance with the recommendations provided under the code. It will also rationalize and consolidate the corporate governance reporting requirements.

The contribution of other stakeholders in the sustainability of companies is now well recognized. It is also the area that Philippine PLCs scored the lowest. Companies should be encouraged to report on their economic, environmental, and/or social impacts that will also articulate their contributions to the sustainable development goals. This will address the increasing focus of foreign investors on the sustainability of the companies. In this regard, the Code of Corporate Governance for PLCs recommends that companies adopt a globally recognized framework in reporting sustainability and non-financial issues.

PHILIPPINES

Table 6.1:   Philippines—in ASEAN Top PLCs
(From the Top 100 PLCs according to Market Capitalization)

Top 50 based on the 2019 ACGS assessment in domestic and regional levels (in alphabetical order)				
1	2GO GROUP, INC.	★		
2	ABOITIZ EQUITY VENTURES, INC.			
3	ABOITIZ POWER CORPORATION			
4	ABS-CBN CORPORATION			
5	ASIA UNITED BANK CORPORATION			
6	AYALA CORPORATION	★		
7	AYALA LAND, INC.	★	★	★
8	BANK OF THE PHILIPPINE ISLANDS	★		
9	BDO UNIBANK, INC.	★		
10	BELLE CORPORATION	★		
11	CEBU HOLDINGS, INC.			
12	CENTURY PACIFIC FOOD, INC.			
13	CHINA BANKING CORPORATION	★	★	★
14	D&L INDUSTRIES, INC.			
15	DMCI HOLDINGS, INC.	★		
16	EAGLE CEMENT CORPORATION			
17	FAR EASTERN UNIVERSITY, INC.			
18	FIRST GEN CORPORATION			
19	GLOBE TELECOM, INC.	★	★	★
20	GT CAPITAL HOLDINGS, INC.	★		
21	INTEGRATED MICRO-ELECTRONICS, INC.			
22	INTERNATIONAL CONTAINER TERMINAL SERVICES, INC.			
23	LOPEZ HOLDINGS CORPORATION			
24	MANILA ELECTRIC COMPANY	★		
25	MANILA WATER COMPANY, INC.			
26	MAX'S GROUP, INC.			
27	MEGAWIDE CONSTRUCTION CORPORATION	★		
28	METRO PACIFIC INVESTMENTS CORPORATION			
29	METROPOLITAN BANK & TRUST COMPANY	★		
30	NICKEL ASIA CORPORATION			
31	PETRON CORPORATION			
32	PHILEX MINING CORPORATION			
33	PHILIPPINE NATIONAL BANK	★		
34	PHILIPPINE SAVINGS BANK			
35	PHILIPPINE SEVEN CORPORATION			
36	PLDT, INC.	★		
37	PREMIUM LEISURE CORP.	★		

continued on next page

Table 6.1 *continued*

Top 50 based on the 2019 ACGS assessment in domestic and regional levels (in alphabetical order)			
38	PXP ENERGY CORPORATION		
39	RIZAL COMMERCIAL BANKING CORPORATION		
40	SAN MIGUEL CORPORATION		
41	SAN MIGUEL FOOD AND BEVERAGE, INC.		
42	SBS PHILIPPINES CORPORATION		
43	SECURITY BANK CORPORATION		
44	SEMIRARA MINING AND POWER CORPORATION	★	
45	SHAKEY'S PIZZA ASIA VENTURES, INC.		
46	SM INVESTMENTS CORPORATION	★	
47	SM PRIME HOLDINGS, INC.	★	★
48	THE PHILIPPINE STOCK EXCHANGE, INC.		
49	UNION BANK OF THE PHILIPPINES		
50	WILCON DEPOT, INC.		

Legend:

★ ASEAN Top 20.

★ ASEAN Asset Class.

★ Country Top 3.

Source: Institute of Corporate Directors Philippines.

PHILIPPINES

SINGAPORE

Corporate Governance Regime

As a leading global financial centre, Singapore places great importance on a consistently high standard of corporate governance to help strengthen investors' confidence in her capital markets. In seeking to maintain global best practices, Singapore adopts a balanced corporate governance ecosystem, balancing between mandatory rules and best practice recommendations.

The Companies Act (CA) is the central legislation that regulates the rights, powers, and liabilities of all Singapore-incorporated companies (private and public). It addresses, among others, the duties of directors and the rights of shareholders. The CA is complemented by case law and judicial pronouncements in areas such as directors' responsibilities.

Local- and foreign-incorporated corporations and other entities (such as real estate investment trusts and business trusts) listed on the Singapore Exchange (SGX) are required to comply with the SGX's listing rules: the Mainboard listing rules for entities listed on the SGX Mainboard, or the Catalist listing rules for smaller growth corporations listed on the sponsor-supervised Catalist listing platform.

The listing rules are given statutory force by the Securities and Futures Act (SFA). The SFA also deals with a range of issues relevant to public-listed entities, such as market conduct and obligations pertaining to disclosure of interests in the securities of listed entities, among others.

The Code of Corporate Governance (CG Code) sets the benchmark for corporate governance best practices in Singapore. The latest version of the CG Code was introduced in 2018 and came into effect in January 2019. Unlike previous iterations of the CG Code, compliance by listed entities with the 13 principles of the CG Code are mandatory. The provisions of the CG Code relating to each principle continue to apply on a "comply or explain" basis. In addition, practice guidance has been issued, which provides guidance on the application of the principles and provisions. Adoption of the practice guidance is voluntary. Among the many revisions made in the slimmed-down 2018 version of the CG Code are the inclusion of a provision that companies should disclose their board diversity policy in their annual report, including measurable objectives and progress made, and a new principle on engagement with stakeholders, requiring the board to adopt an inclusive approach in considering and balancing the needs and interests of material stakeholders. Based on the latest ACGS assessment for 2019, a sizable proportion of listed entities have already adopted many of the practices prescribed by the CG Code.

Major amendments to the SGX's listing rules were introduced in 2018 and 2020. Among the 2018 amendments were the introduction of a listing framework for dual class share (DCS) structures, clarification of certain categories of directors as non-independent, and the introduction of mandatory training requirements for first-time listed entity directors. One of the more contentious amendments was the inclusion of a rule that directors would not be independent if they have been directors for an aggregate period of more than 9 years (whether before or after listing), and their continued appointment as independent directors has not been sought and approved in separate resolutions: one, by all shareholders; and another, by shareholders excluding the directors and CEO and their respective associates. This much-debated rule will come into effect on 1 January 2022, together with a new rule hardwiring the requirement that the board comprise at least one-third independent directors. In addition, in 2020, after a lengthy consultation, the SGX made quarterly reporting non-mandatory for all listed entities other than those with an adverse auditors' opinion.

Various regulators, including Singapore Exchange Regulation (SGX RegCo) which was established in September 2017 to undertake all of SGX's regulatory functions, the Monetary Authority of Singapore (MAS), the Accounting and Corporate Regulatory Authority of Singapore, and the Commercial Affairs Department of the Singapore Police, play a part in the enforcement of the various laws and regulations and the SGX listing rules.

On 12 February 2019, the Corporate Governance Advisory Committee, a standing industry-led body, was set up by the MAS to advocate good corporate governance practices among listed entities in Singapore.

On the whole, Singapore, with its well-balanced corporate governance ecosystem and a reputation for strict enforcement, has been consistently ranked at the top in having a well-maintained corporate governance regime in the region by the Asian Corporate Governance Association in its CG Watch, which assesses the quality of corporate governance in the Asia and Pacific markets. This ongoing external independent assessment and continued internal monitoring by various stakeholders ensures that Singapore's corporate governance regime remains effective and relevant and continues to support business growth and innovation in a continually disruptive global business environment.

Scorecard Assessment for Companies

The ASEAN Corporate Governance Scorecard (ACGS) was developed based on the G20/OCED Principles of Corporate Governance that recommends the adoption of most common global corporate governance best practices in major international business markets. The group has made a continued effort over the years to incorporate the latest developments in corporate governance and raise its rigor of assessment. Additionally, questions relating to more important practices have also been given additional weightage within each part in Level 1. New questions have been added to the Bonus section to reflect the aspirational aspects of this scorecard while some practices that have become the minimum standard expected of listed companies in ASEAN have been moved from the Level 2—i.e., the Bonus section to Level 1—to reflect the continued improvements in corporate governance practices in the region.

The methodology and assessment criteria for 2019 followed the revised scorecard in the prior assessment period where more in-depth assessment questions were added to cover issues relating to important practices so that companies are incentivized to raise their disclosure standards on corporate governance practices in their annual reports and corporate websites.

For the assessment year of 2019, a list of the Top 100 Singapore companies by market capitalization as of 31 March 2019 was drawn up for the assessment. These 100 companies with a combined market capitalization of S$484.04 billion accounted for 49.9% of SGX's total market capitalization of S$969.14 billion. As in earlier assessments, to make the process more rigorous, the top 35 companies identified from each participating country after the domestic assessment were randomly selected for peer review by the domestic ranking bodies of the other five participating countries. At the end of the peer review, a list of the top performing companies in ASEAN was drawn up for further discussion and finalization by all participating domestic ranking bodies. For 2019, all companies in ASEAN that achieved a minimum score of 97.5 points (75% of the total 130 points achievable), the top 20 companies in ASEAN, and the top 3 companies in each jurisdiction were identified. For Singapore, 5 of its companies were ranked in the top 20 in ASEAN, while 26 of its companies achieved the minimum score of 97.5 points.

SINGAPORE

Key Findings

Singapore publicly listed companies (PLCs) showed significantly improved performance in ACGS 2019. As indicated above, more than a quarter (26) of the companies scored at least 97.5 points out of a maximum of 130 (75% of the total attainable points), while 5 of its companies were ranked in the Top 20 ASEAN PLCs.

Overall, Singapore PLCs attained an average score of 88.3 out of the maximum of 130 points in 2019, compared to an average score of 78.5 in 2017. Likewise, the average score for Level 1 increased significantly by 7.4 from 73.5 in 2017 to 80.9 in 2019. This suggests that Singapore PLCs have made good progress in improving their corporate governance practices and in making more relevant disclosures.

Table 7.1:   Singapore—Average Total Scores and Average Level 1 Scores

Year	Max Total Score	Total Score Range	Average Total Score	Average Level 1 Score (Out of 100)
2015	126	49.0–116.0	78.1	74.6
2017	130	46.4–120.0	78.5	73.5
2019	130	66.0–119.7	88.3	80.9

Source: Singapore Institute of Directors and Centre for Governance and Sustainability, NUS Business School.

Figure 7.1:   Singapore—Distribution of Companies by Total Scores

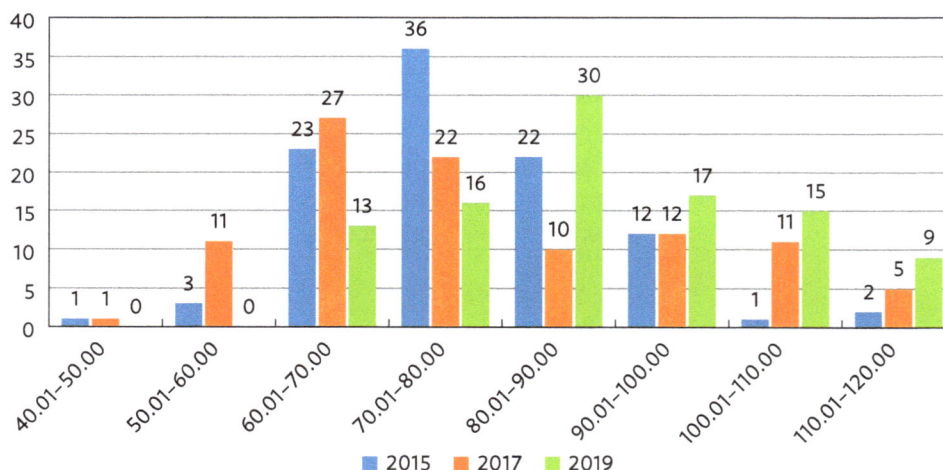

Source: Singapore Institute of Directors and Centre for Governance and Sustainability, NUS Business School.

Figure 7.1 shows the total score distribution of the top 100 PLCs between 2015 and 2019. It shows that the proportion of companies in the higher total score interval of 80.01–120.00 increased significantly over the 5-year period. For example, there were only two companies in the interval of 110.01–120.00 in 2015. By 2019, there was more than a threefold increase to nine companies in the same range. Equally important, no companies were in the lower range of 40.01–60.00 in 2019. This demonstrates an across-the-board improvement in the total scores of the top 100 PLCs over the period.

The top 10 Singapore PLCs with the highest total scores arranged in alphabetical order are City Developments Ltd, ComfortDelGro Corp Ltd, DBS Holdings Ltd, Keppel Corp Ltd, Oversea-Chinese Banking Corp Ltd, SATS Ltd, Singapore Exchange Ltd, Singapore Press Holdings Ltd, Singapore Telecommunications Ltd, and United Overseas Bank Ltd.

Comparison of Average Scores for Level 1

The annual ACGS results of Singapore PLCs are compared based on Level 1 scores, which are out of 100 points, and Level 1 and Level 2 scores combined even though the weightages for individual questions have been revised over the years. The average scores for Level 1 increased steadily from 56.5 in 2012 to 80.9 in 2019 except for a marginal dip in 2017 (Table 7.2). This represented a 43.2% improvement in Level 1 scores over a 7-year period. The marginal dip may be due to the increased complexity of the questionnaire when it was reviewed and revised in 2016.

Table 7.2:   Singapore—Level 1 Scores

Year	Average Score for Level 1 (out of 100)
2012	56.5
2013	65.1
2014	67.0
2015	74.6
2017	73.5
2019	80.9

Source: Singapore Institute of Directors and Centre for Governance and Sustainability, NUS Business School.

Scores by Component

Figure 7.2 provides a detailed breakdown of the normalized Level 1 scores for the period 2012 to 2019. Singapore PLCs performed uniformly much better across all sections over the years. As a new methodology was introduced, resulting in the change in weightage of Part B from 15% to 10% and Part C from 10% to 15%, the scores in the corresponding parts were normalized to better reflect the time trends. In addition, there were also changes in the weightage for some individual questions. In fact, the points allocated to some questions were doubled.

Among the sections, the greatest improvement was in Part C. There was an increase of 114% from 5.7 in 2012 to 12.2 in 2019 in the scores of Part C—Role of Shareholders. Part B—Equitable Treatment of Shareholders had the smallest rise in the scores, registering 19% increase from 7.8 to 9.3 over the same period. Since the inception of the study, the improvements in scores for all the remaining three parts were significant: Part A—Rights of Shareholders (69%), Part D—Disclosure and Transparency (42%), and Part E—Responsibilities of the Board (41%).

Rights of Shareholders

Singapore has a comprehensive regulatory framework to enhance the participation and protection of rights of shareholders. Singapore PLCs are expected to continue to diligently observe this aspect of corporate governance. On the whole, Singapore PLCs have performed well. However, there are still areas for improvement as identified.

Figure 7.2:   Singapore—Normalised Level 1 Scores by Section

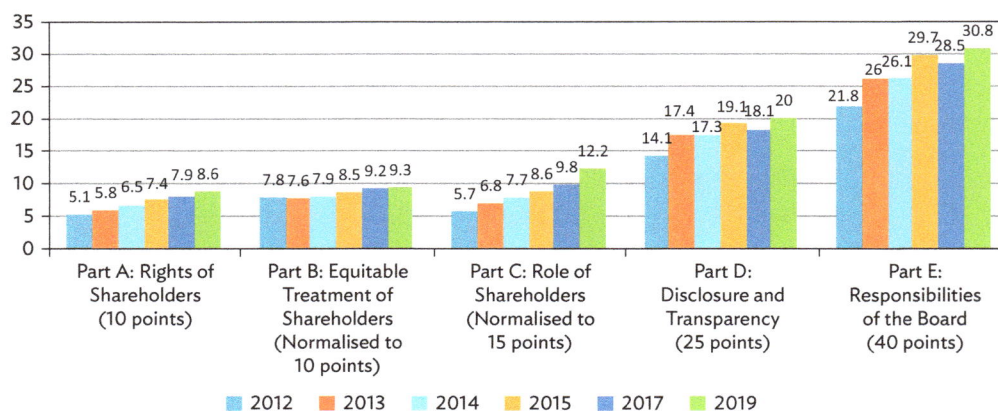

Source: Singapore Institute of Directors and Centre for Governance and Sustainability, NUS Business School.

Part A: Rights of Shareholders

Strengths

- All PLCs disclosed that shareholders had the opportunity, evidenced by an agenda item, to approve remuneration (fees, allowances, benefit-in-kind, and other emoluments) or any increases in remuneration for the non-executive directors.

- All PLCs allowed shareholders to elect directors individually.

- All PLCs allowed voting in absentia.

- All PLCs made publicly available by the next working day the result of the votes taken during the most recent annual general meeting (AGM) for all resolutions.

- All PLCs voted by poll (as opposed to by show of hands) for all resolutions at the most recent AGM.

- Almost all PLCs provided the rationale and explanation for each agenda item that required shareholders' approval in the notice of AGM/circulars and/or the accompanying statement.

Areas for Improvement

- More PLCs should disclose the list of board members including the CEO (if not a board member) who attended the most recent AGM.

- More PLCs should publish their minutes of the AGM on their company websites and the minutes of the most recent AGM should record that the shareholders were given the opportunity to ask questions and the questions raised by shareholders and answers given recorded.

- More PLCs could have paid (interim and final/annual) dividends in a timely manner; that is, all shareholders are paid within 30 days after being (i) declared for interim dividends and (ii) approved by shareholders at general meetings for final dividends.

- More Singapore PLCs should provide at least 21 days of notice for all AGMs and extraordinary general meetings.

Equitable Treatment of Shareholders

The SGX's listing rules and the CG Code place great emphasis on the rights of shareholders and, above all, the fair and equitable treatment of all shareholders. This section deals with matters relating to common shareholders' rights, among other things, voting rights, insider trading, and related party transactions (RPTs).

Singapore PLCs demonstrated their efforts in treating their shareholders fairly and equitably, evidenced by adherence to the "one-share-one-vote" principle by companies. One-share-one-vote structure, considered by many proponents as the bedrock of corporate governance standards, will continue to be the default structure for companies listed in Singapore. Since the amendment to the CA and revision to the listing rules, companies are now able to offer shares with multiple voting rights and suitable companies with DCSs can be listed on the SGX.

Despite the controversy over the DCSs, the unique structure may protect entrepreneurial management from short-termism of the market and help them concentrate in pursuing the long-term strategic goals of the company. The DCS listings will also broaden investment options for seasoned investors who can fully comprehend the risks and business model associated with such listings. The listing rules for companies with such DCSs have also incorporated adequate protection for all shareholders including founding shareholders.

The continued updating and revision of regulations and best practices in Singapore's balanced corporate governance ecosystem and ensuring equitable treatment for all shareholders have continued to enhance investor confidence in Singapore's standing as a leading global capital market.

After the revision of the scorecard in 2016, the weightage of this section was reduced to 10% from 15%. Overall, Singapore PLCs performed better over the years, albeit the rate of increase was the smallest among all sections.

Part B: Equitable Treatment of Shareholders

Strengths

- All PLCs did not have bundling of items in resolutions for AGMs.
- All directors and employees were prohibited from benefiting from insider information not generally available to the market.
- Almost all companies reported the dealings of their directors in company shares within the stipulated regulatory period.
- Almost all PLCs reported that they had a policy requiring directors to disclose their interest in transactions and any other conflicts of interests.
- Most PLCs made their proxy documents easily available.

SINGAPORE

Areas for Improvement

- More PLCs should have a disclosed policy requiring board members and directors to abstain from participating in the board discussion on any particular agenda when they are conflicted.
- More PLCs should disclose whether their RPTs are conducted in such a way to ensure that they are fair and at arm's length.
- More PLCs should disclose the full profiles of directors (at least age, academic qualification, date of appointment, experience, and directorships in other listed companies) seeking election/re-election in their notice of AGM/circulars.

Role of Stakeholders

A network of symbiotic relationships exists between Singapore PLCs and their stakeholders. As business entities do not function in a vacuum, business decisions made by corporations will have impacts on the stakeholders and society as a whole and vice versa. This is especially so when production value chains have become globalized, even though existing infrastructures would have to be reviewed and revised in the light of the disruptions caused by the COVID-19 pandemic. Further to this, investors and stakeholders have also become increasingly assertive and demanding accountability from business entities in running a responsible and sustainable business.

Against this backdrop, in 2017, SGX implemented a set of new listing rules requiring listed companies to produce a sustainability report which must describe the sustainability practices with reference to the primary components, such as material environmental, social, and governance factors, sustainability reporting framework, and board statement, just to name a few. The new listing rules will be enforced on a "comply or explain" basis, which means that for any primary component that a company fails to report on, it must state so and explain what it does instead and the reasons for doing so. In the revised 2018 CG Code, companies are encouraged to consider and balance the needs and interests of material stakeholders, as part of the board's overall responsibility to ensure that the best interests of the company are served.

After the revision of the ACGS Scorecard in 2016, this section was given increased weightage from 10% in the previous framework to 15% in the new framework in the 2017 assessment, thus reflecting and acknowledging the increasing importance of stakeholder engagement. On the whole, almost all Singapore PLCs published a separate report/section that discussed their efforts on environment, economic, and social issues. Equally important, a significant number of them also had a comprehensive whistle-blowing policy in place.

Part C: Role of Shareholders

Strengths

- All PLCs reported their efforts to interact with the communities and to keep their value chain environmentally friendly.
- All except one PLC published a separate report/section that discussed their efforts on environment/ economic and social issues.
- Almost all PLCs published relevant information on training and development programs for their employees.
- A significant number of PLCs have a comprehensive whistle-blowing policy in place.

Areas for Improvement

- More Singapore PLCs should disclose their supplier/contractor selection and criteria.
- More Singapore PLCs should disclose their anti-bribery and anti-corruption policies and practices.
- More PLCs should have clear procedures on how to protect an employee/person who reveals alleged illegal/unethical behavior from retaliation.

Part D: Disclosure and Transparency

Timely release of material information of companies to investors is essential in building investor confidence. This section provides a comprehensive coverage on material disclosures investors need in order to make informed decisions. After a slight decline in the average score in 2017 due to the more stringent requirements in the revised scorecard, the average score significantly improved in 2019 as a result of greater efforts by PLCs to improve their disclosure practices.

Singapore PLCs should continue to enhance their disclosures in their annual reports and on their websites. Companies should also publish minutes of AGMs on their company websites on a timely basis. More PLCs could also consider providing a link to their company's constitution on their websites.

Strengths

- All PLCs released the audited annual financial reports within 120 days from the financial year end.
- All PLCs disclosed the direct and indirect (deemed) shareholdings of directors.
- All except one PLC disclosed attendance details of each director in all board and board committee meetings held during the year.
- All PLCs' board of directors and/or the relevant officers of the companies provided affirmation for the true and fair representation of the annual financial reports.
- Almost all PLCs disclosed details of their parent/holding companies, subsidiaries, associates, joint ventures, and special purpose enterprises/vehicles.
- Almost all PLCs provided financial performance indicators.

Areas for Improvement

- More PLCs could consider providing a link to their company's constitution on their websites.
- More Singapore PLCs should disclose non-financial performance indicators and their dividend policy in annual reports.
- More PLCs should disclose the direct and indirect (deemed) shareholdings of senior management.
- More PLCs should publish AGM minutes on their corporate websites and on a timely basis.
- More PLCs should disclose full biographical details (at least age, academic qualifications, date of first appointment, relevant experience, and any other directorships of listed companies) of all directors.

SINGAPORE

Part E: Responsibilities of the Board

As the Code of Corporate Governance puts significant emphasis on board responsibilities, this is mirrored in the 40-point weightage of this section. This section assesses aspects of board-related matters, including board duties and responsibilities, structure, process, and performance.

The revised 2018 CG Code strengthened the focus on board responsibilities, independence, and renewal. Some major changes include requiring two-tiered shareholder vote to approve the appointment of independent directors who have served beyond 9 years and lowering the threshold of 10% to 5% of total voting rights for eligibility to demand a poll. In addition, the SGX's listing rules require that independent directors must form at least one-third of the board by 2021, while the revised 2018 CG Code recommends that in the event of the chair being non-independent, independent directors shall comprise a majority of the board. Companies are also required to have non-executive directors forming the majority of their board. They are also expected to disclose their board diversity policy including measurable objectives.

Singapore PLCs generally performed well in this section as attested by an increase of 41% in the average scores by 8 points from 21.8 in 2012 to 30.8 in 2019. For instance, all Singapore PLCs disclosed that they had established a sound internal control procedures/risk management framework and periodically reviewed the effectiveness of that framework. All annual reports also contained a statement by their boards and audit committees on the adequacy of the companies' internal controls/risk management systems. Further to that, all except one Singapore PLC had their audit committee comprised entirely of non-executive directors, with the chair and a majority comprising independent directors.

However, there are still areas for improvement. Chief among them is that more Singapore PLCs should disclose the annual performance assessment of their CEO conducted by their board of directors. In addition, more Singapore PLCs should also provide disclosure on the process of their annual performance assessment of individual directors in their annual reports.

Strengths

- All Singapore PLCs had independent directors as the chair in their audit committee.
- All Singapore PLCs disclosed that they had established a sound internal control procedures/risk management framework and periodically reviewed the effectiveness of that framework.
- All Singapore PLCs disclosed that the board of directors and audit committees had conducted reviews of the company's material controls (including operational, financial, and compliance controls) and risk management systems.
- All Singapore PLCs included in their annual report a statement from the board of directors or audit committee commenting on the adequacy of the company's internal controls/risk management systems.
- All except one Singapore PLC clearly stated the roles and responsibilities of their chair and board of directors.
- All except one Singapore PLC disclosed the types of decision requiring board of directors' approval.

- All except one Singapore PLC had their audit committee comprised entirely of non-executive directors with the chair and a majority comprising independent directors.

- All except two Singapore PLCs disclosed that their board of directors had approved the remuneration of the executive directors and/or the senior executives.

- Most PLCs stated that they had conducted an annual performance assessment of the board of directors and disclosed the criteria and process followed for the assessment.

- Most Singapore PLCs had at least 50% of independent directors on boards and committees.

Areas for Improvement

- More Singapore PLCs should disclose the annual performance assessment of their CEO conducted by their board of directors.

- More Singapore PLCs should provide disclosure of the process for the annual performance assessment of individual directors.

- More Singapore PLCs should disclose the process concerning how the board plans for the succession of the CEO and key management.

- Singapore PLCs should disclose more details on their code of ethics and conduct, and how they monitor compliance with this code.

- More Singapore PLCs should set a term limit of 9 years or less for directors.

- More Singapore PLCs should have measurable standards to align the performance-based remuneration of the executive directors and senior executives with long-term interests of the company.

- More Singapore PLCs should consider setting a limit of five board seats that an individual independent/non-executive director may hold concurrently.

- More Singapore PLCs should ensure that the board papers for board of directors' meetings are provided to the board at least 5 business days in advance of the board meeting.

Table 7.3:   Singapore—Average Bonus and Penalty Scores

Year	Average Bonus Score	Average Penalty Score	Average Level 2 Score
2015	6.7	3.2	3.5
2017	8.5	3.6	4.9
2019	11.3	3.9	7.4

Source: Singapore Institute of Directors and Centre for Governance and Sustainability, NUS Business School.

The Level 2 section of the scorecard comprises bonus and penalty questions. The aim is to encourage companies to adopt best practices and to penalize them for breaches of regulation and good corporate governance practices. Following revision of the scorecard in 2016, there is a greater emphasis on board diversity, board independence, and governance processes around information technology (IT) issues. Table 7.3 shows that the average bonus score increased from 6.7 in 2017 to 11.3 in 2019 even though the average penalty score also increased from 3.2 to 3.9 over the same period. Overall, there was an increase in the average score for Level 2 from 3.5 to 7.4.

In line with the call for greater board diversity, more Singapore PLCs had at least one female independent director. Although Singapore PLCs generally had a board diversity policy, more companies should disclose measurable objectives for implementing its policy and report on progress in achieving its objectives. More companies should release their notice of AGM (with detailed agendas and explanatory circulars) at least 28 days before the date of the meeting. Further to that, more companies should also have their audited annual financial report/ statement released within 60 days of their financial year end. The board can also improve the disclosure of their risk oversight by providing more details in their annual reports on their governance processes around IT issues including disruption, cyber security, and disaster recovery so as to ensure that all key risks are identified, managed, and reported to the board.

On the whole, most Singapore PLCs performed well in areas related to board composition and responsibilities. However, an area of concern is that a sizable number of Singapore PLCs had independent directors serving for more than 9 years. Such practice will reduce board independence of the companies.

Conclusions

Singapore PLCs significantly improved their performance in 2019. More than a quarter (26) of the companies scored at least 97.5 points out of a maximum of 130. Five Singapore PLCs were ranked in the Top 20 ASEAN PLCs. Overall, Singapore PLCs attained an average score of 88.3 out of the maximum score of 130 points in 2019 compared to an average score of 78.5 in 2017. In a nutshell, Singapore PLCs have steadily progressed in providing increased disclosures of their corporate governance practices. They also performed uniformly much better across all sections over the years, with the section on the Role of Shareholders registering the greatest increase of 114% over the 7-year period.

There are many key strengths in the corporate governance practices of Singapore PLCs. All PLCs made disclosures in the following areas: all directors and employees were prohibited from benefiting from insider information not generally available to the market; all Singapore PLCs disclosed that their company had established a sound internal control procedures/risk management framework and periodically reviewed the effectiveness of that framework.

However, some key areas of improvement are required to raise the state of corporate governance to the next level. For example, more PLCs should have a disclosed policy requiring board members to abstain from participating in the board discussion on any particular agenda where they are conflicted. Further to that, they should disclose and address their anti-bribery and corruption policies and practices. More PLCs should also publish AGM minutes on their corporate websites. Disclosure concerning annual performance assessment of the CEO conducted by their board of directors and of individual directors should also be provided.

With the revised 2018 CG Code coming into full effect by 2021, this will allow companies latitude in articulating their corporate governance practices in their annual reports to comply with the spirit and intent of the code rather than just the letter of it. We believe that this emphasis on substance over form will help to further improve the state of corporate governance in Singapore PLCs in the future.

Table 7.4:   Singapore Top 50 Companies in 2019 by Ranking
(Based on Public Disclosures Available as of July 2019)

S/No.	Top 50 PLCs	Top 3 Singapore PLCs	Top 20 ASEAN PLCs	ASEAN Asset Class*
1	SATS LTD.	★	★	★
2	SINGAPORE EXCHANGE LIMITED	★	★	★
3	UNITED OVERSEAS BANK LIMITED	★	★	★
4	OVERSEA-CHINESE BANKING CORPORATION LIMITED		★	★
5	SINGAPORE TELECOMMUNICATIONS LTD		★	★
6	CAPITALAND LIMITED			★
7	CITY DEVELOPMENTS LIMITED			★
8	COMFORTDELGRO CORPORATION LTD			★
9	DBS GROUP HOLDINGS LTD			★
10	FAR EAST ORCHARD LIMITED			★
11	FRASER AND NEAVE LIMITED			★
12	FRASERS PROPERTY LIMITED			★
13	GREAT EASTERN HOLDINGS LIMITED			★
14	HONG LEONG ASIA LTD.			★
15	KEPPEL CORPORATION LIMITED			★
16	OLAM INTERNATIONAL LIMITED			★
17	PERENNIAL REAL ESTATE HOLDINGS LIMITED			★
18	SBS TRANSIT LTD			★
19	SEMBCORP INDUSTRIES LTD			★
20	SEMBCORP MARINE LTD			★
21	SIA ENGINEERING COMPANY LIMITED			★
22	SINGAPORE AIRLINES LTD			★
23	SINGAPORE POST LIMITED			★
24	SINGAPORE PRESS HOLDINGS LTD			★
25	SINGAPORE TECHNOLOGIES ENGINEERING LTD			★
26	STARHUB LTD.			★
27	BUKIT SEMBAWANG ESTATES LIMITED			
28	CHINA AVIATION OIL (SINGAPORE) CORPORATION LTD			
29	DELFI LIMITED			
30	FIRST RESOURCES LIMITED			
31	GENTING SINGAPORE LIMITED			
32	GUOCOLAND LIMITED			
33	HAW PAR CORPORATION LIMITED			
34	HI-P INTERNATIONAL LIMITED			
35	HO BEE LAND LIMITED			

Table 7.4:   ASEAN Corporate Governance Scorecard in 2019–2020 (*continued*)

S/No.	Top 50 PLCs	Top 3 Singapore PLCs	Top 20 ASEAN PLCs	ASEAN Asset Class*
36	HONG LEONG FINANCE LIMITED			
37	JARDINE CYCLE & CARRIAGE LIMITED			
38	RAFFLES MEDICAL GROUP LTD			
39	ROXY-PACIFIC HOLDINGS LIMITED			
40	SHENG SHIONG GROUP LTD.			
41	SILVERLAKE AXIS LTD			
42	THAI BEVERAGE PUBLIC CO LTD			
43	THOMSON MEDICAL GROUP LIMITED			
44	TUAN SING HOLDINGS LIMITED			
45	UNITED INDUSTRIAL CORPORATION LIMITED			
46	VENTURE CORPORATION LIMITED			
47	VICOM LTD			
48	WILMAR INTERNATIONAL LIMITED			
49	YEO HIAP SENG LTD			
50	YOMA STRATEGIC HOLDINGS LTD.			

Note: * ASEAN Asset Class refers to the class of companies in ASEAN that achieved a minimum score of 97.5 points (75% of the total 130 points achievable) in the ASEAN Corporate Governance Scorecard in 2019.

Source: Singapore Institute of Directors and Centre for Governance and Sustainability, NUS Business School.

SINGAPORE

Development of the Corporate Governance Framework

Sustainable development of capital markets is an important mission of a regulatory agency. The Thai capital markets and institutional investors in Thailand have recently placed more emphasis on sustainable investment. Disclosure of business operations involving the environment, social, and governance (ESG) dimensions linking to the company's financial performance is thus a must. The Securities and Exchange Commission, Thailand (SEC) has attended to the importance of ESG and published the Corporate Governance Code for Listed Companies 2017 (CG Code). An aim is to be a practical guideline for boards of directors in applying corporate governance to achieve good long-term performance and value for sustainable investment. In 2017, the SEC also distributed the Investment Governance Code for institutional investors to use as a guideline for internationally accepted investment management.

In 2019, the SEC was well aware of the UN Guiding Principles on Business and Human Rights (UNGPs) which directs emphasis to protect, respect, and remedy—and thus applied this UN framework to business and human rights with the listed companies. The SEC believes that if the business sector applies this UN framework, it will enhance the companies' risk management, business operations, and human rights to achieve the UN's Sustainable Development Goals. On 29 October 2019, the Cabinet of Thailand authorized the SEC to commence the National Agenda Plan on Business and Human Rights. Thailand was the first country in Asia to initiate this national business and human rights plan.

To tentatively be effective in 2021, the SEC determines that the chair of the board and chief executive officer (CEO) must not be the same person (no CEO duality) for companies issuing shares to the public. The Stock Exchange of Thailand may also apply this code to the listed companies.

The Thai Institute of Directors was assigned by the SEC to be a domestic ranking body to develop and review assessment criteria in the ASEAN CG Scorecard (ACGS) and disseminate the knowledge to Thai listed companies. The ACGS training and seminars received a warm welcome from the listed companies and hence equipped them to effectively apply the governance principles. As a result, Thailand has exhibited a continuous improvement in the average ACGS score.

Overall Analysis

The overall average score for Thai listed companies was 96.60 points in 2019, an increase by 10.87 points from 2017 (Table 8.1). The maximum score was 118.90 points compared to 115.37 in 2017.

For the scores in each category, Thai listed companies exhibited an improvement in the average scores in all categories (Table 8.2). The Rights of Shareholders and Equitable Treatment of Shareholders categories showed an increase in the average scores because 99 out of 100 companies had made the English annual general meeting (AGM) minutes publicly available. For the Role of Stakeholders category, an improvement in substance over form resulted in a score increase. In the Disclosure and Transparency category, the companies had made all directors' profiles and the websites more informative to enhance the average score in this category. The Responsibilities of the Board category also showed an improvement in average score, especially from the disclosure of the roles and responsibilities of the board of directors, sub-committees, and chair.

Table 8.1:   Thailand—Overall Performance

Year	2012	2013	2014	2015	2017	2019
ASEAN Total Score (points)	**117**	**142**	**128**	**126**	**130**	**130**
Maximum	85.95	104.17	104.60	104.60	115.37	118.90
Average	67.7	75.39	84.53	87.53	85.73	96.60
Minimum	43.45	46.03	62.68	62.68	30.63	69.38

Source: Thai Institute of Directors.

Table 8.2:   Thailand—Performance by Categories

Part	Year	Rights of Shareholders	Equitable Treatment of Shareholders*	Role of Stakeholders*	Disclosure and Transparency	Board Responsibilities
Average Score (Level 1 only)	2012	8.33	14.48	5.12	17.39	22.67
	2013	8.62	14.24	5.64	17.17	22.60
	2014	9.19	14.51	7.38	19.06	28.35
	2015	9.06	14.75	8.09	20.07	29.68
	2017	8.93	**9.79**	**11.84**	20.69	28.91
	2019	9.61	**9.94**	**13.66**	22.53	32.08

* The original scores on the Equitable Treatment of Shareholders and Role of Stakeholders in 2012–2015 are weighted 15% and 10%, respectively. The new scores on the Equitable Treatment of Shareholders and Role of Stakeholders in 2017–2019 are 10% and 15%, respectively.
Source: Thai Institute of Directors.

Performance by Score Range

Of 100 sample companies, a majority of Thai listed companies were in the 90–99 score range in 2019 (Table 8.3). For top performers relative to 2017, Thai listed companies demonstrated an improvement in corporate governance practices, evident by an increase of 16 companies in the 100-or-above score range in 2019.

Table 8.3: Thailand—Performance by Score Intervals

Range of Score	Number of Companies					
	2012	2013	2014	2015	2017	2019
100 and upper	–	4	5	15	18	34
90–99	–	13	29	30	19	39
80–89	11	16	32	24	35	22
70–79	34	30	31	24	13	4
60–69	37	27	3	7	10	1
50–59	14	8	–	–	3	–
40–49	4	2	–	–	1	–
30–39	–	–	–	–	1	–
Total Companies	**100**	**100**	**100**	**100**	**100**	**100**

Source: Thai Institute of Directors.

Performance by Industry Sector

In 2019, Thai listed companies exhibited an improvement in the average scores in all industry sectors (Table 8.4). The top three sectors were energy and utilities, technology and telecommunication, and industry sectors. The healthcare sector showed a significant score increase from 2017, even though this sector showed the lowest average scores in 2 consecutive years. Thus, more effort to improve the corporate governance practices in the healthcare sector is in order.

Table 8.4: Thailand—Performance by Industry Sector

Industry Sector	2012	2013	2014	2015	2017	2019
Energy and Utilities	70.55	81.08	86.23	91.47	87.63	101.45
Technology and Telecommunication	72.77	82.99	91.22	98.30	94.19	100.63
Industry	66.71	67.21	79.56	85.51	85.16	98.90
Finance	69.35	85.54	90.97	90.87	88.90	96.57
Consumer Services	68.24	74.00	83.42	84.25	83.76	95.78
Property	–	71.86	81.47	83.65	88.43	92.10
Consumer Goods	66.45	68.72	82.31	82.53	85.27	92.08
Healthcare	61.52	61.11	75.43	73.00	56.81	89.74

Source: Thai Institute of Directors.

Performance by Market Capitalization

This report classifies listed companies into four size groups: companies with a large market capitalization of ฿600,000–1,000,000 million; those with a market capitalization of ฿100,000–599,999 million; those with a market capitalization of ฿60,000–99,999 million; and those with a market capitalization of ฿10,000–59,999 million.

THAILAND

THAILAND

Table 8.5 shows the corporate governance performance of companies by their market capitalization. In general, the higher the market capitalization, the higher the average scores. In 2019, companies in the ฿100,000–599,999 million, ฿60,000–99,999 million, and ฿10,000–59,999 million showed improved average scores while companies in the ฿600,000 and above showed slightly decreased average scores.

Table 8.5: Performance by Market Capitalization

Range of Market Capitalization (฿ million)	2012	2013	2014	2015	2017	2019
600,000 and above	74.97	93.4	97.45	101.35	106.99	105.76
100,000–599,999	74.63	79.33	89.15	92.50	92.66	101.85
60,000–99,999	70.77	80.08	85.10	91.55	82.84	96.04
10,000–59,999	66.81	71.80	82.25	84.06	81.37	93.53
Lower than 10,000	60.30	–	–	–	–	–

Source: Thai Institute of Directors.

Part A: Rights of Shareholders

The Rights of Shareholders principle aims to assess whether the company recognizes the shareholders' rights in its business affairs. A well-governed firm must ensure that shareholders' rights are well facilitated. Shareholders should be able to exercise their ownership rights, including the right to receive dividends, participate in the AGM, and elect the directors, among others.

The average score in the Rights of Shareholders category was 9.61 points in 2019, a slight increase from 8.93 points in 2017. Thai listed companies showed good practices on disclosing the voting and vote tabulation procedures before the AGM proceedings and a disclosure of the vote by poll for all AGM resolutions, and also recording the shareholders' questions and answers for each agenda clearly. These aforementioned governance practices imply that the listed companies paid attention to the rights of shareholders at the AGM. Moreover, in 2019, there was an improvement on appointment of an independent party to validate the votes at the AGM, which increased from 75% in 2015 to 91% in 2017.

In terms of areas for improvement, Thai listed companies need to provide better disclosure of directors' all benefit-in-kind (in addition to the regular retainer fees, meeting allowance, and bonuses) for shareholders' approval at the AGM. Also, the disclosure of all board members and the CEO attending the AGM need to be further improved. Even though the percentages of companies earning scores in these areas rose since 2015, there is still room for improvement.

Strengths

- Companies disclose voting and vote tabulation procedures used, declaring before the meeting proceeds as well as the vote by poll (as opposed to a show of hands) for all resolutions at the most recent AGM.
- Companies disclose that the AGM minutes show that there is an opportunity for shareholders to ask questions, and all questions and answers are recorded in the AGM minutes.
- Companies disclose that they appoint an independent party (scrutineers/inspectors) to count and validate the votes at the AGM.

Areas for Improvement

- All forms of director remuneration should be proposed for shareholders' approval in the AGM.
- All board members and the CEO (if not a board member) need to attend the most recent AGM.

Part B: Equitable Treatment of Shareholders

The Equitable Treatment of Shareholders addresses whether minority (non-controlling) shareholders are treated fairly and equally alongside the controlling shareholders. The AGM process, for example, should enable all shareholders to participate in the meeting without undue complexity. Also, outside shareholders should be protected from possible actions such as tunneling by the controlling shareholders acting directly or indirectly through the use of material nonpublic information and related party transactions (RPTs).

The average score of the equitable treatment of shareholders category in 2019 was 9.94 points which is higher than 9.79 points in 2017. The strength under this category is the quality of notice to call an AGM, especially in clearly identifying the auditors who are seeking appointment/re-appointment. In addition, Thai listed companies also disclose whether their RPTs were conducted in a fair manner and at arm's length, which shows a steady improvement from 87 points in 2017 to 98 in 2019.

There is still a lack of the information on candidate directors with respect to the date of their first appointment and directorship in other listed companies. The proportion of companies earning a score in this criterion continuously improves.

Strengths

- Disclosure of profiles of auditors seeking appointment or re-appointment is clearly identified.
- Companies disclose that RPTs are conducted in such a way to ensure that they are fair and at arm's length.

Areas for Improvement

- Companies should disclose information about date of first appointment and directorship(s) in other publicly listed companies of individuals seeking director election or re-election in the notice of call to AGM.

Part C: Role of Stakeholders

The Role of Stakeholders principle concentrates on the issues of corporate social responsibilities to all stakeholders. The goal is to encourage a corporate responsibility through the company's activities in relation to the environment, consumers, business partners, competitors, employees, communities, creditors, and other stakeholders. This category examines the company's policies and practices pertaining to the acknowledgment and treatment of their related stakeholders.

The average score for the role of stakeholders in 2019 was 13.66 points, an increase of 11.84 points from 2017. The improvement is found year-on-year in disclosure of the practices, such as supplier/contractor selection procedures, production process under environmental regulation, promoting sustainable development, anti-corruption programs, and contact details for stakeholders to voice their concerns regarding the company. In addition, details on employee welfare and details on training and development programs (statistics, average training hours, number of

THAILAND

employees attending programs, courses' expense, and courses' names) are clearly disclosed. Thai listed companies also provide more information on the procedures on a whistle-blowing policy and the protection for persons who reveal unethical behavior from retaliation.

Areas for improvement for Thai listed companies are the disclosure of their governance practices pertaining to the protection of creditor's rights and compensation policy for employees linked to short-term and long-term corporate performance.

Strengths

- Companies disclose clear practices dealing with supplier selection.
- Companies disclose clear activities regarding environmental standards and sustainability.
- Companies clearly disclose their anti-bribery and anti-corruption policy and practices.
- Companies provide contact details via the company's website or annual report, which stakeholders (e.g., customers, suppliers, and general public) can use to voice their concerns and/or complaints concerning possible violation of their rights.
- Companies disclose clear practices dealing with employees' health, safety, and welfare.
- Companies publish relevant information on training and development programs for their employees.
- Companies have a comprehensive whistle-blowing policy in place.
- Companies have policy or procedures to protect an employee or individual who reveals illegal/unethical behavior from retaliation.

Areas for Improvement

- Practices dealing with creditors' rights safeguarded should be disclosed clearly.
- Policies related to reward or compensation that account for the performance of the company beyond short-term financial measures should be clearly disclosed.

Part D: Disclosure and Transparency

The Disclosure and Transparency principle concerns the accuracy, completeness, and punctuality of corporate information disclosure. Companies should disclose material corporate information in a timely and cost-effective manner through a variety of channels to reach all interested and relevant parties. The firm's ownership structure, RPTs, and financial and non-financial information are all significant items to disclose.

The 2019 results for this category improved from 20.69 points in 2017 to 22.53 in 2019. Overall, Thai listed companies disclose all required information relating to biographical details of all directors and management, and non-financial performance indicators more clearly.

The strength in this area is an improvement of adequately incorporated fundamental information in the annual report, such as the identity of the beneficial owners of substantial shareholders, the information on each director (date of first appointment and directorship in other listed companies by showing separately between listed and non-listed companies), and the disclosure of directors' shareholdings at the beginning and end of the year. Additionally, Thai listed companies disclose the audit and non-audit fees, and evidence of the analyst's briefings.

Nonetheless, there is still much room for improvement in this area. Companies need to improve disclosure on non-financial information such as long-term corporate objectives, market share, and reasons for non-compliance issues. Other improvement opportunities that need to be made are the disclosure of dividend policy, media briefings/press conferences, and posting the company's constitution on its website.

Strengths

- Companies disclose the identities of all beneficial owners holding more than 5% of issued shares.
- Companies disclose biographical details (at least age, academic qualifications, date of first appointment, relevant experience, and any other directorships of listed companies) of all directors/commissioners.
- Companies disclose trading in the company's shares by insiders.
- Companies disclose the audit and non-audit fees.
- Companies disclose the evidence of analyst's briefings conducted.

Areas for Improvement

- The corporate objectives and non-financial performance indicators should be disclosed in the annual report.
- Dividend policy should be disclosed more clearly.
- The annual report should contain a statement confirming the company's full compliance with the code of corporate governance and, where there is non-compliance, identify and explain reasons for each such issue.
- The evidence of actual media briefings/press conferences conducted during the year under review should be disclosed.
- Company's constitution (company's by-laws, memorandum, and articles of association) should be disclosed on the company's website.

Part E: Responsibilities of the Board

The Responsibilities of the Board focus on the duties, responsibilities, and accountabilities of the board of directors to the shareholders and other stakeholders. By taking into account the interests of all stakeholders, the board of directors must apply high ethical standards to the business to effectively fulfill their responsibilities. The board is mainly responsible for guiding corporate strategy, monitoring managerial performance, and preventing conflicts of interest.

This category assesses the development of corporate strategy, monitoring of the business operations, and pledge of transparent business practices, presence of proper financial control and reports, procedures for director nomination, orientation of new board members, board performance evaluation, and search process and evaluation of the CEO, among others.

The average score in 2019 of 32.08 points increased from 28.91 points in 2017. In terms of a key success area, an increasing number of Thai listed companies put more emphasis on the disclosure of the types of decisions requiring board of directors' approval. Encouraging practices are that all directors, senior management, and employees are required to comply with the code of conduct, together with the effective implementation and monitoring of the code. There are clear statements about how the board of directors manage any business key risks and comment on the adequacy of the company's internal controls and risk management systems. Further, there are more details

THAILAND

of criteria used in selecting new directors and more details on the new directors' orientation. Moreover, scores improve for an annual board of directors' and individual directors' assessment.

Items that remain a challenge for Thai listed companies are disclosure of the processes on review, and monitoring and overseeing the implementation of corporate strategy. The board of directors' structure should comprise at least 50% independent directors. Moreover, the board of directors should set the term limit of 9 years for independent directors, the limit of 5 board seats for an independent director, the 75% minimum of meeting attendance of each director, the requirement of a minimum quorum of at least two-thirds for board decisions, and the independence of chair of the board. For the audit committee, the responsibility for recommendation on the appointment and removal of the external auditor should be clearly disclosed. In terms of company secretary, he/she must keep abreast of the relevant program every year—Thai listed companies show only 42% achievement for this criterion. There is also room for improvement in the short-term and long-term remuneration policy for the CEO, the process of the CEO succession plan, and annual assessment of the CEO and all board sub-committees.

Strengths

- Companies disclose the types of decisions requiring board of directors' approval.
- Companies disclose that all directors, senior management, and employees are required to comply with the code. Also, companies disclose the implementation and the monitoring of the code of ethics or conduct.
- Companies clearly disclose the criteria used in selecting new directors.
- The key risks to which the company is materially exposed to (i.e., financial, operational including IT, environmental, social, and economic) are disclosed clearly.
- Companies contain a statement from the board of directors commenting on the adequacy of the company's internal controls/risk management systems.
- Companies disclose the roles and responsibilities of the chair.
- Companies have orientation programs for new directors and provide clear details of the programs.
- Companies conduct annual performance assessment of the board of directors and the individual directors, which disclose the criteria and process followed for the assessment.

Areas for Improvement

- Companies should state that the board of directors monitors and oversees the implementation of the corporate strategy.
- Independent directors should make up at least 50% of the board of directors.
- Companies should set the policy on the term limit of 9 years for independent directors.
- Companies should set a limit of five board seats that an individual independent/non-executive director may hold simultaneously.
- Each of the directors should attend at least 75% of all the board meetings held during the year.
- Companies should set the policy on the minimum quorum requirement of at least two-thirds for board decisions.

- The non-executive directors of the company should meet separately at least once during the year without any executives present. Also, the purpose of the meeting and issues discussed must be stated.

- The chair should be an independent director.

- The audit committee should have responsibility for recommendation on the appointment, and removal of the external auditor.

- The company secretary should be trained in legal, accountancy, or company secretarial practices and be abreast of relevant developments.

- Companies should disclose the remuneration (fees, allowances, benefit-in-kind, and other emoluments) policy/practices in both short-term and long-term incentives and performance measures for the CEO.

- Companies should disclose the process on the succession plans of the CEO.

- The board of directors should conduct annual performance assessment of the CEO and all board sub-committees.

Bonus and Penalty

The bonus and penalty criteria are discussed separately in this section. The purpose of the bonus items is to recognize companies that go beyond the minimum corporate governance practices as required in Level 1. In contrast, a penalty is recorded for companies with governance practices or violations that are beyond the pale of the good corporate governance paradigm.

In general, Thai listed companies have improved bonus points in all sections. An increasing number of companies release the notice of AGM at least 28 days before the date of the meeting, and distribute their audited annual financial statements within 60 days from the financial year end. Almost all Thai listed companies show that the chair of the board, audit committee chair, and CEO attend the most recent AGM.

Nonetheless, there is much room for improvement in this area. Thai listed companies need to consider to adopt an internationally recognized reporting framework for sustainability, e.g., Global Reporting Initiative (GRI). Also, the companies should appoint at least one female independent director in the board and the nomination committee needs to entirely comprise independent directors to earn the bonus point. The board of directors should undertake a process of identifying the quality of directors that aligns with the company's strategic directions. The use of professional search firms or other external sources of candidates when searching for candidates to the board of directors is recommended. The establishment of a separate board-level risk committee and setting a governance policy on IT issues are also recommended to enhance the company's best practices.

Strengths

- The notice of the AGM, as announced to the Stock Exchange, is released at least 28 days before the date of the meeting. (Bonus)

- The audited annual financial report or statement is released within 60 days from the financial year end. (Bonus)

- The chair of the board, audit committee chair, and CEO attend the most recent AGM. (Penalty)

THAILAND

Areas for Improvement

- Companies should adopt an internationally recognized reporting framework for sustainability (e.g., GRI).
- Companies should have at least one female independent director. (Bonus)
- The nominating committee should entirely comprise independent directors. (Bonus)
- Companies should disclose that the nomination committee undertakes the process of identifying the quality of directors aligned with the company's strategic directions. (Bonus)
- Companies should use professional search firms or other external sources of candidates when searching for candidates to the board of directors. (Bonus)
- The board should describe its governance process around IT issues including disruption, cyber security, and disaster recovery, to ensure that all key risks are identified, managed, and reported to the board. (Bonus)
- Companies should have a separate board-level risk committee. (Bonus)

Conclusions and Recommendations

Overall, Thai listed companies have continued to strengthen good corporate governance over the years by stressing the importance of both form and substance. There is a higher quality of policies and practices pertaining to the stakeholders in terms of the customers' welfare, supplier selection procedures, creditors' rights, and anti-corruption programs—together with clear disclosure of the company's code of ethics and the implementation compliance with the code. Thai listed companies also pay much attention to the business's key risks (financial, IT, environment, social, and economic) by clearly disclosing both policy and practices on this issue.

Thai listed companies also attach importance to the ESG and GRI framework, even though the score did not much improve. In regard to establishing a risk management committee, Thai listed companies had a slightly increased score—this remains one of the challenges for improvement in many Thai listed companies.

Table 8.6:   Thailand—Top 50 PLCs
(in alphabetical order)

No.	Company Name			
1	ADVANCE INFO SERVICE PUBLIC COMPANY LIMITED		★	
2	AIRPORTS OF THAILAND PUBLIC COMPANY LIMITED		★	
3	AMATA CORPORATION PUBLIC COMPANY LIMITED		★	
4	ASIA AVIATION PUBLIC COMPANY LIMITED			
5	BANGCHAK CORPORATION PUBLIC COMPANY LIMITED	★	★	★
6	BANGKOK AVIATION FUEL SERVICES PUBLIC COMPANY LIMITED		★	
7	BANK OF AYUDHYA PUBLIC COMPANY LIMITED		★	
8	CENTRAL PATTANA PUBLIC COMPANY LIMITED		★	
9	CHAROEN POKPHAND FOODS PUBLIC COMPANY LIMITED		★	
10	COL PUBLIC COMPANY LIMITED		★	
11	EASTERN WATER RESOURCES DEVELOPMENT AND MANAGEMENT PCL.		★	
12	ELECTRICITY GENERATING PUBLIC COMPANY LIMITED		★	
13	GLOBAL POWER SYNERGY PUBLIC COMPANY LIMITED		★	
14	GUNKUL ENGINEERING PUBLIC COMPANY LIMITED		★	
15	HANA MICROELECTRONICS PUBLIC COMPANY LIMITED		★	
16	HOME PRODUCT CENTER PUBLIC COMPANY LIMITED		★	
17	INDORAMA VENTURES PUBLIC COMPANY LIMITED		★	
18	INTOUCH HOLDINGS PUBLIC COMPANY LIMITED		★	
19	IRPC PUBLIC COMPANY LIMITED		★	
20	KASIKORNBANK PUBLIC COMPANY LIMITED		★	
21	KCE ELECTRONICS PUBLIC COMPANY LIMITED		★	
22	KIATNAKIN BANK PUBLIC COMPANY LIMITED		★	
23	KRUNG THAI BANK PUBLIC COMPANY LIMITED		★	
24	KRUNGTHAI CARD PUBLIC COMPANY LIMITED		★	
25	LH FINANCIAL GROUP PUBLIC COMPANY LIMITED		★	
26	MINOR INTERNATIONAL PUBLIC COMPANY LIMITED		★	
27	MUANGTHAI CAPITAL PUBLIC COMPANY LIMITED		★	
28	PLAN B MEDIA PUBLIC COMPANY LIMITED		★	
29	PRECIOUS SHIPPING PUBLIC COMPANY LIMITED		★	
30	PRUKSA HOLDING PUBLIC COMPANY LIMITED		★	
31	PTG ENERGY PUBLIC COMPANY LIMITED			
32	PTT EXPLORATION AND PRODUCTION PUBLIC COMPANY LIMITED	★	★	
33	PTT GLOBAL CHEMICAL PUBLIC COMPANY LIMITED		★	
34	PTT PUBLIC COMPANY LIMITED	★	★	★
35	RATCHABURI ELECTRICITY GENERATING HOLDING PUBLIC COMPANY LIMITED		★	
36	ROBINSON PUBLIC COMPANY LIMITED			
37	SAHA PATHANA INTER-HOLDING PUBLIC COMPANY LIMITED			

THAILAND

Table 8.6:   Thailand—TOP 50 PLCs (*continued*)

No.	Company Name			
38	SIAM CITY CEMENT PUBLIC COMPANY LIMITED			
39	SINGHA ESTATE PUBLIC COMPANY LIMITED		★	
40	STAR PETROLEUM REFINING PUBLIC COMPANY LIMITED			
41	THAI AIRWAYS INTERNATIONAL PUBLIC COMPANY LIMITED		★	
42	THAI OIL PUBLIC COMPANY LIMITED	★	★	★
43	THAI VEGETABLE OIL PUBLIC COMPANY LIMITED		★	
44	THE SIAM CEMENT PUBLIC COMPANY LIMITED		★	
45	THE SIAM COMMERCIAL BANK PUBLIC COMPANY LIMITED		★	
46	TISCO FINANCIAL GROUP PUBLIC COMPANY LIMITED		★	
47	TMB BANK PUBLIC COMPANY LIMITED			
48	TOA PAINT (THAILAND) PUBLIC COMPANY LIMITED		★	
49	TOTAL ACCESS COMMUNICATION PUBLIC COMPANY LIMITED		★	
50	TRUE CORPORATE PUBLIC COMPANY LIMITED			

Remark: ROBINSON PUBLIC COMPANY LIMITED was voluntarily delisted from the Stock Exchange of Thailand effective 20 February 2020.

Legend:

★ ASEAN Top 20.

★ ASEAN Asset Class.

★ Country Top 3.

Source: Thai Institute of Directors.

VIET NAM

Background of the Corporate Governance Framework

In Viet Nam, the legal frameworks that lay the foundation for corporate governance enforcement and oversight are available from the Enterprise Law, the Securities Law, and the Information Disclosure Regulations. The recent revision of the Enterprise Law 2014 set out important recommendations for new governance models to be applied in Viet Nam. Also, Decree 71/2017/ND-CP and Circular 95/2017/TT-BTC replace previous regulatory documents in promulgating legal regulations on corporate governance for publicly listed companies (PLCs), along with Decree 05/2019/ND-CP regulating the role of internal audit responsibilities. The recently issued Law on Enterprises in 2020 improves corporate governance regulations, especially in terms of the role of an audit committee. This new regulation will become effective in 2021.

Compared with other stock markets in the ASEAN region with a long history of capital market development, the presence of these important legal documents indicates that the Vietnamese stock market has been equipped with a full fundamental legal background on corporate governance and is ready for regional and global integration. The year 2019 also marks an important time when Viet Nam had its first Corporate Governance Code (CG Code) that sets out the guidelines for PLCs toward quickly applying national corporate governance standards, and is expected to help improve the quality of corporate governance in Vietnamese enterprises in the coming years. One emphasis of the CG Code is on the corporate governance structure and roles and responsibilities of the board. The CG Code is expected to hasten PLCs adopting the international corporate governance principles.

With established grounded legal frameworks, how to enforce the rules and promote good governance principles in corporate practices is perhaps the biggest challenge in Viet Nam. With more than 750 PLCs, the total capitalization of Viet Nam's stock market was ₫3,568,624 billion as of 31 October 2019, equivalent to $153 billion, or 58% of GDP; it is clear that Viet Nam's stock market has great potential for growth. However, the quality and development potential of the market depends greatly on the quality of corporate governance, especially on the role of the corporations in regard to their shareholders, which is the very first concern of investors when deciding to invest capital in a market.

The Vietnam Institute of Directors (VIOD) was nominated by the SSC to be the DRB of Viet Nam to conduct the ACGS assessment for 2019 and the years to come. VIOD is a professional organization which promotes corporate governance standards and best practices in the Vietnamese corporate sector. VIOD aims to advance board professionalism, promote business ethics and transparency, create a pool of independent directors, build a network to connect corporate leaders and stakeholders, and help companies gain investor confidence.

Overall Analysis

There were 82 companies in the assessment of 2019 that met the reviewing criterion of disclosing investor documents in English. Compared to 70 companies being assessed in 2017, the number of reviewed companies increased by 17% as more companies were recognized as having key investor information publicly disclosed in English. This is a very encouraging signal, which means that more companies are now responsive to providing equitable treatment to foreign investors in information disclosure and transparency. In the 2019 assessment, the reviewed companies were large-scale firms with a total market capitalization of $116 billion, equivalent to 76% total market capitalization of Viet Nam, being a good sample representing the companies in the stock market of Viet Nam.

Figure 9.1:   Improvement of CG Score over the 2 Years

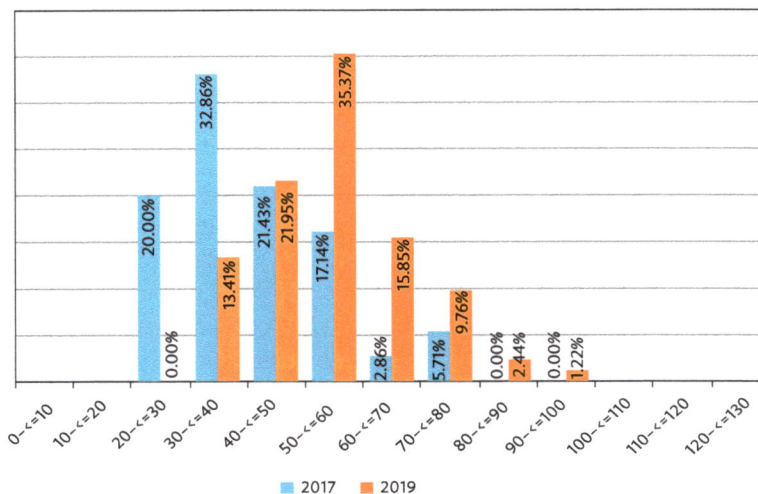

Source: Viet Nam Institute of Directors.

Overall, there was an improvement of corporate governance disclosures and practices since the previous assessment (Figure 9.1). Companies scored higher in 2019 compared to 2017, with 35.37% of firms scoring 50–60 points (on the 130-point scale), and about 30% of firms scoring above 60 points. The best company in Viet Nam, Viet Nam Dairy Products Joint Stock Company (with stock code: VNM), scored above 97.5 points (or above the 75% threshold score) and received an ASEAN Assess Class award.

Figure 9.2:   Overall Corporate Governance Performance of Viet Nam over the Assessment Years

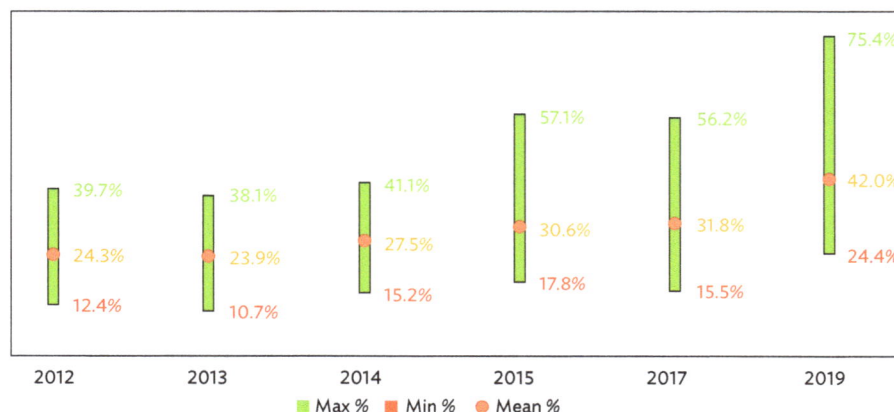

Source: Viet Nam Institute of Directors.

Figure 9.2 shows the percentage score, a relative scale to the maximum score, of Vietnamese PLCs reviewed in 6 continuous years of assessment. In 2019, the corporate governance score of Vietnamese PLCs was an average of 41.7%, a significant increase from 31.8% in 2017. The maximum and minimum scores also improved significantly compared to 2017 and previous years, showing solid and remarkable improvement in corporate governance of Vietnamese companies.

Table 9.1:   Corporate Governance Score of Vietnamese PLCs Over the 6 Assessment Years

Assessment Year	2012	2013	2014	2015	2017	2019
Number of Firms Reviewed	39	40	50	55	70	82
Maximum Possible Score (points)	117	142	128	120	130	130
Maximum Score of PLCs (points)	46.5	54.1	52.6	68.5	73.1	98.0
Minimum Score of PLCs (points)	14.5	15.2	19.5	21.4	20.2	31.7
Median Score of PLCs (points)	27.8	31.0	33.8	34.7	38.7	54.0
Mean Score of PLCs (points)	28.4	33.9	35.1	36.8	41.3	54.6

Source: Viet Nam Institute of Directors.

Table 9.1 shows the corporate governance performance in a point scale, the mean score of 2019 was 54.6 points—a significant improvement from 41.3 points in 2017. The maximum score increased to 98.0 points from 73.1 in 2017. These improvements are encouraging, and show that Viet Nam is constantly improving in corporate governance both in firm practices and in regulatory frameworks. The enhancement of regulations and enforcements has shown clear outcomes.

Figure 9.3:   Improvements in Corporate Governance Practices in Each Area

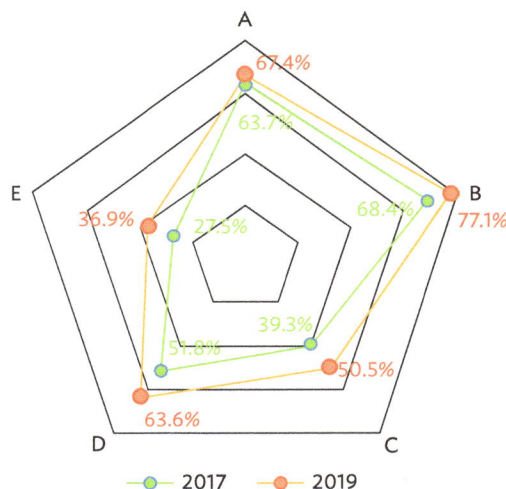

Source: Viet Nam Institute of Directors.

Comparing the improvement of the five aspects of corporate governance for 2019 versus 2017 shows that the greatest improvements are in Roles of Stakeholders (Part C), Disclosure and Transparency (Part D), and Responsibilities of the Board (Part E) (Figure 9.3). Although being among the most improved areas, boards' responsibilities in corporate governance are still a concern for Vietnamese PLCs with their average score far below the ASEAN average (score 36.9% in 2019). Board responsibility is very important for corporate governance of a firm and, therefore, the poor board responsibility explains the relatively poorer performance in corporate governance of Vietnamese PLCs compared to their peers in other jurisdictions. Among the areas, Rights of Shareholders (Part A) and Equitable Treatment of Shareholders (Part B) are strictly regulated areas and score relatively well.

Enterprises in high growth and well-managed industries are always attractive to investors. Investors pay special attention to companies in industries with large capitalization, high liquidity, and most importantly good governance. Figure 9.4 shows corporate governance score of each industry sector on the y-axis (on the x-axis is the liquidity of stocks of the sector, measured by stock trading volume in 2019), with the size of the bubbles representing the size of firms in the sector (measured by market capitalization in 2019). The number in the bracket next to the name of the sector is the number of companies reviewed in the industry. The most attractive sectors for investment with good governance in Viet Nam are consumer goods, pharmaceutical and health, finance, banking, and consumer services.

Figure 9.4:   Liquidity, Market Capitalization, and Corporate Governance of Sectors in 2019
(Market capitalization represented by size of bubbles)

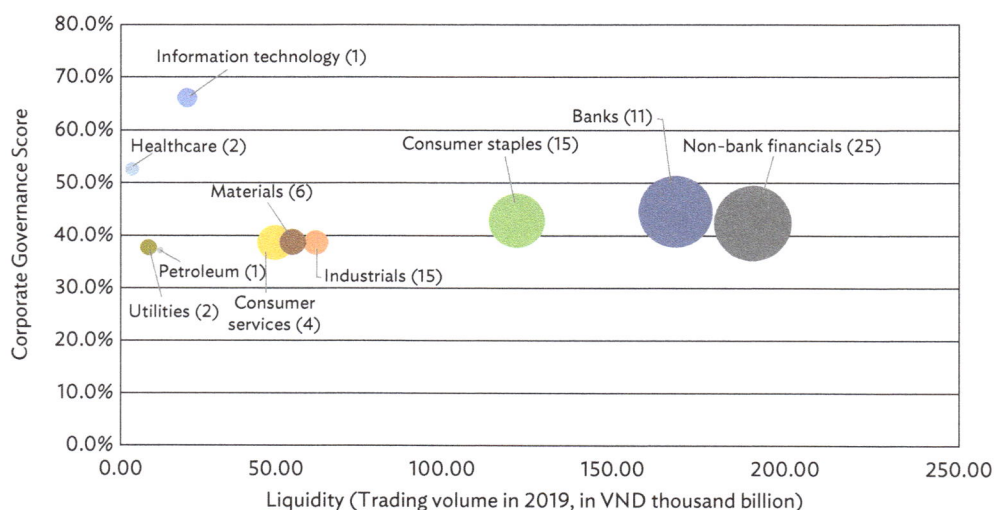

Source: Viet Nam Institute of Directors.

Enterprises with good business performance often attract investors' capital, are able to receive good technology from investors, and have advantages in increasing scale. However, to achieve profitable and sustainable development, the quality of corporate governance is a compelling factor to retain investors for the long-term development of the company. The sectors with superior operating efficiency and good corporate governance in Viet Nam are pharmaceuticals and healthcare, information technology, and consumer goods (Figure 9.5). These sectors have relatively high return on assets, good scale, and correspondingly good corporate governance.

Figure 9.5:   Corporate Governance, Firm Performance, and Firm Size in Sectors
(Firm size represented by size of bubbles)

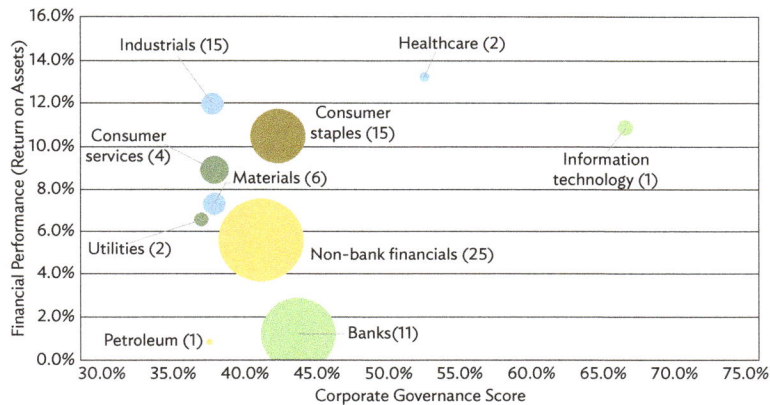

Source: Viet Nam Institute of Directors.

Performance of Corporate Governance in Each Area

Over the 6 years of assessments, Vietnamese PLCs have improved corporate governance practices in each of the corporate governance areas, showing consistent efforts in each aspect of corporate governance. This part will analyze the specific practices of corporate governance and its strengths and areas for improvement.

Figure 9.6:   Six Areas of Corporate Governance over the Assessment Years

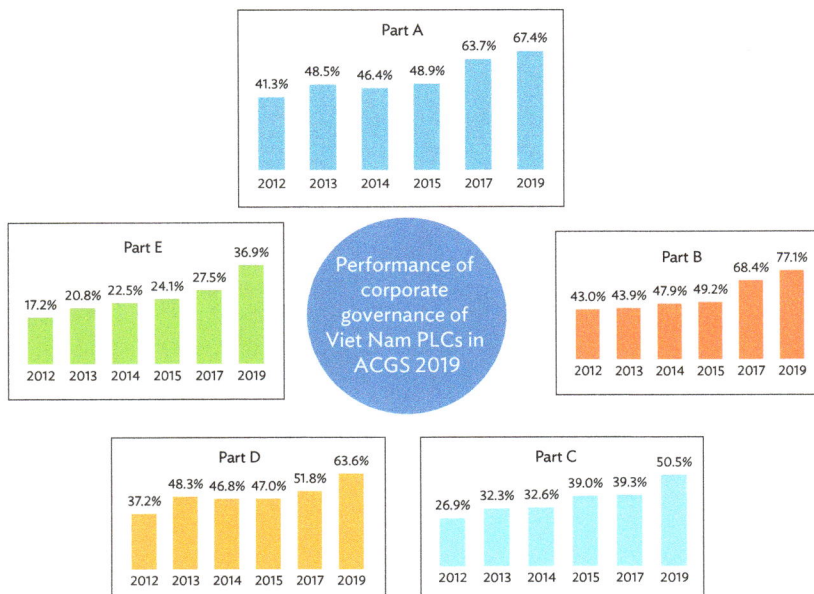

Source: Viet Nam Institute of Directors.

Part A: Rights of Shareholders

Rights of Shareholders (Part A) is among the best performing areas of corporate governance for Vietnamese PLCs, with 67.4% of criteria in Level 1 being met (Figure 9.6). Rights of shareholders are well regulated by sets of regulations in Viet Nam and strictly monitored by the regulators. Therefore, in general, Vietnamese PLCs perform well in regulated areas of rights of shareholders. Specifically, more and more improvements have been seen in pre-annual general meeting (AGM) preparation, detailed disclosure of AGM resolutions before and after the AGMs, procedures and organization of shareholder meetings, and voting procedures in AGM. Moreover, PLCs have become more aware of the importance of shareholder engagement and more active in attracting investment capital and boosting the business reputation in various investor interaction opportunities.

However, there is a need for further improvement in timely payment of dividends to meet the ASEAN standards, which require cash dividends to be paid within 30 days and stock dividends to be paid within 60 days after being announced or approved by AGM. Improvements are also expected in sending out AGM invitations early and in providing informative minutes of AGMs/extraordinary general meetings (EGMs) with more detail on the question and answer section.

Strengths

- More companies actively engage with shareholders beyond the AGMs
- Much improvement in disclosing and explaining each AGM resolution

Areas for improvement

- Very few companies paying dividends promptly
- Not very much disclosure on AGMs for contents of question and answer sessions
- Few companies send out invitations 21 days before AGMs and EGMs

Part B: Equitable Treatment of Shareholders

Equitable Treatment of Shareholders (Part B) is the best performing area of corporate governance principles for Vietnamese PLCs (Figure 9.6), with 77.1% of criteria met in 2019—an increase from 68.4% in 2017. Companies publish more shareholder documents in English for the benefit of foreign investors. More comprehensive and more efficient company websites being available in English was an apparent improvement in 2019.

However, improvements are expected in such key areas as process to nominate new directors. This is an area that affects equitable treatment of minority and non-controlling shareholders who have limited information about the new candidates. Information on the new candidates not only must meet comprehensive requirements of the ASEAN standards but also needs to be circulated well early prior to the AGMs. A second area of attention is information on related party transactions. While this is a well-regulated area, quality of information on value, nature of the transactions, and whether it is assured that the transactions are fair and at market arm's length are still shortcomings.

Strengths

- More companies provide AGM documents in English comprehensively and promptly

Areas for improvement

- Very few companies provide comprehensive profiles of new candidates of the board of directors
- Very limited disclosure that related party transactions are fair and at market arm's length

Part C: Roles of Stakeholders

Part C was among the most improved areas in 2019, in which Vietnamese PLCs met 50.5% of ASEAN criteria (Figure 9.6). Improvements have been seen in relation to customer welfare, such as product quality, health and safety of customers, and after sales services. Companies are more actively achieving sustainable development goals, with 90% of companies showing their commitment with various policies and activities to build an environmentally friendly value chain for sustainable development, and to be active in solving economic and social issues.

Despite improvements, Part C is still a challenging area for Vietnamese PLCs mainly due to limited disclosure on such sensitive areas as supplier and contractor selection procedures, and employee reward or compensation policy, that accounts for company performance beyond short-term financial measures, and policies and practices to safeguard creditors' rights. Other areas are still new to PLCs in Viet Nam such as anti-corruption programs and whistle-blowing policy, which require stronger enforcement and encouragement from both the regulators and the market.

Strengths

- More companies apply practical policies to address customers' welfare
- Most companies devote effort to ensure that the value chain is environmentally friendly, promoting sustainable development
- Most companies well describe their efforts on environment, economy, and social issues
- Most companies commit to allocate effort to interact with the surrounding communities

Areas for improvement

- Very few companies disclose supplier and contractor selection procedures
- Very few companies disclose policies to safeguard creditors' rights
- Not many companies have a reward or compensation policy that accounts for the performance of the company beyond short-term financial measures
- Very few companies disclose policies and exercise anti-corruption programs and procedures
- There are very few companies with a whistle-blowing policy to report alleged illegal and unethical behavior

Part D: Disclosure and Transparency

Part D was the most improved area in corporate governance practices of Vietnamese PLCs in the 2019 assessment, where 63.6% of criteria were met, an increase from 51.8% in the previous assessment (Figure 9.6). Improvements have been seen in better timeliness of disclosing financial statements, better quality of annual reports, better website quality, more transparency of ownership structure, and more disclosure of non-financial performance.

VIET NAM

Improvements are expected in providing information or evaluation on the independence of external auditors, especially in cases where the external auditor provides non-audit services as well as the audit service. Companies in Viet Nam have not been very active in providing objective judgment of the financial analysts about its activities, and have not posted respective media briefings and press conference contents on their websites. Although there has been improvement in disclosure of information on name, relationship, nature, and value of material-related party transactions (RPTs), there is limited disclosure concerning companies' policies on reviewing and approving material RPTs to avoid conflicts of interest.

Strengths

- The majority of companies provide non-financial performance indicators
- Majority of companies disclose name, relationship, nature, and value for each material RPT

Areas for improvement

- Not many companies disclose policies covering the review and approval of material RPTs
- Very few companies disclose audit and non-audit fees, and very little information to verify how external auditors' independence is exercised
- Not much information on media briefings or press conferences is provided on company websites
- Not all companies provide articles of association on their website

Part E: Responsibilities of the Board

Part E is the most important area of corporate governance, but is also the most challenging area for Vietnamese PLCs. There was a large increase in score in 2019, meeting 36.9% of the criteria of the ASEAN standards from a score of 27.5% in the previous assessment; however, this does not make this area a safe one for Vietnamese PLCs in the journey to more sustainable and better corporate governance without strong leadership from the board of directors. It is observable that improvements are apparently shown in efforts in setting up internal audit function (in 55% of assessed companies), and establishing and periodically reviewing the effectiveness of a risk management framework, which sets a firm background for internal corporate governance of a safer and more sustainable development for firms. Separating the roles of chair and CEO is also an apparent and outstanding effort by Vietnamese PLCs in recent years.

Some key corporate documents, such as corporate governance policies and codes of conducts, have not been disclosed on corporate websites with helpful details. Although many PLCs separate the roles of chair and CEOs (73% of PLCs), very few have an independent chair (6%). Nominating new directors is a very important area but has not received enough attention. Orientation and training programs for new directors and directors in place have not been well practiced and disclosed (only 20% of PLCs).

Although boards of directors in Viet Nam play a leading role in the process of developing and reviewing the companies' strategies, information regarding their activities in monitoring and overseeing the implementation of the corporate strategy is rarely illustrated. In exercising their roles, it is not common for non-executive members of the board to organize a meeting without the presence of executive members.

Prior to the revision of the Law of Enterprise in 2014, in the two-tier board structure of Vietnamese PLCs, the supervisory board assumes many of the roles of an audit committee in a one-tier board structure. There is an important revision component in the Law of Enterprise regarding board structure that recommends companies to establish a strongly independent audit committee in the board of directors. The PLCs are now active in responding to this recommendation, with increasing numbers establishing audit committees in the board of directors to replace or support a supervisory board. However, the independence of the audit committee should be a focal effort in coming years with more non-executive independent members to be nominated to the committee and an independent member to be selected to chair the committee. Board structures in Vietnamese PLCs should be strengthened with more functional committees, such as remuneration committees and nomination committees, being established.

Strengths

- Many companies setting up internal audit function
- Majority of companies have a sound internal control procedures and risk management framework and periodically review its effectiveness
- Most companies separate the chair and CEO positions
- The majority of companies have their board of directors performing well in attending board meetings

Areas for improvement

- Not many companies disclose their corporate governance policies or board charters
- Very few companies provide details of their codes of conduct
- Very few companies have an independent chair
- Very few companies encourage directors to attend ongoing or continuous professional education programs
- Very few companies have an audit committee comprising a majority of independent directors and with an independent chair
- Not many companies have established nomination and remuneration committees
- Not many companies provide detailed information on remuneration of each member of the board of directors
- Very few corporate secretaries are trained in legal, accountancy, or company secretarial practices and are conversant with relevant developments

Bonus and Penalty

Bonus and penalty is a challenging area for companies in Viet Nam (Figure 9.7). However there are also good signals that some companies are more proactive in achieving high ASEAN standards of corporate governance in their practices, with 37.8% of PLCs getting bonus scores for adopting internationally recognized reporting frameworks for sustainability, such as Global Reporting Initiative (GRI), Integrated Reporting (IR), and Sustainability Accounting Standards Board (SASB). In searching for a new director, a few PLCs (5%) have used professional search firms or external sources of candidates. Some PLCs (16%) have policies and implementation to encourage board diversity; 14% of PLCs have at least one female independent director. Some PLCs (25.6%) are very keen on risk management, and have set up a board-level risk committee, and adequately govern IT risk issues, such as disruption, cyber security, and disaster recovery to ensure that all key risks are identified, managed, and reported to the board.

VIET NAM

Figure 9.7:   Corporate Governance Score—Levels 1 and 2

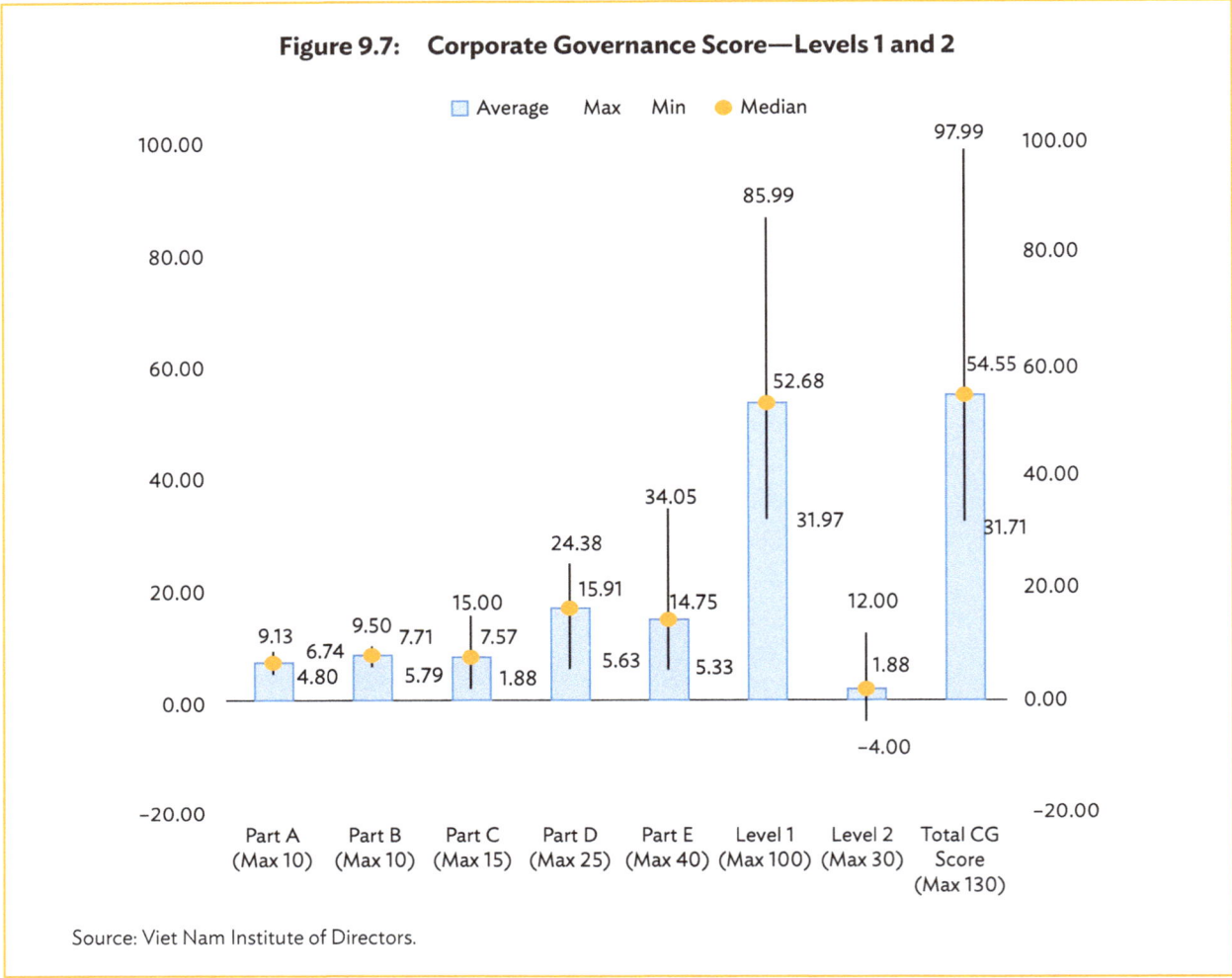

Source: Viet Nam Institute of Directors.

In practicing corporate governance, due to low disclosure, some areas received penalties such as non-disclosure on full presence of the chair, audit committee chair, and CEO at the AGMs, and non-disclosure on the independence status of board members. A number of companies still have a chair cum CEO.

Strengths

- There is a good signal that firms are active in adopting internationally recognized reporting frameworks for sustainability
- A few companies use professional search firms or external sources of candidates for new candidates to the board of directors
- Some companies get bonus scores for providing detailed disclosure of CEO remuneration
- Some companies have policies and disclose measurable objectives for implementing board diversity and report on progress in achieving the objectives
- Some companies have at least one female independent director

- There is a signal that some boards exercise a strong role in governing IT issues including disruption, cyber security, and disaster recovery
- There is an indication that companies are keen on setting up board-level risk committees

Areas for Improvement

- Low disclosure concerning attendance of the chair, audit committee chair, and CEO at the AGM in a few companies
- A few companies fail to identify the independent directors
- Some companies still have the chair as the CEO

Conclusions and Recommendations

The 2019 assessment of Vietnamese PLCs showed significant improvements in all areas of corporate governance as a result of more effort in effective disclosure of shareholder documents in English, with better quality and timeliness of information disclosure. However, a lot more effort is needed to improve corporate governance aspects such as corporate policies and practices toward protecting all stakeholders' values, and especially roles and responsibilities of the board of directors.

In terms of improving stakeholders' values, codes of conduct and whistle-blowing policies should be built, published in detail, and be effectively implemented. These two documents will also form an effective mechanism to safeguard good corporate governance. Regarding the roles and responsibilities of the board of directors, there should be improvements in board structure and composition. More independent directors should be nominated to the board to chair functional committees of the board, such as audit, nomination, and remuneration committees. Board committee charters should be disclosed with clear roles and responsibilities of each committee. Each director of the board should be keen in fulfilling the fiduciary duties in their activities with high integrity. In brief, to improve corporate governance, efforts must come from each PLC, from its governance leaders, the board of directors, and corporate governance supporting units in the PLC, being accompanied by activism of the market.

VIET NAM

Table 9.2: Viet Nam—Top 3 Publicly Listed Companies in the ASEAN Corporate Governance Scorecard Based on 2019 Total Score
(alphabetical order by stock code)

Stock Code	Company Name	ASEAN Asset Class
FPT	FPT CORPORATION	
NVL	NOVALAND GROUP	
VNM	VIET NAM DAIRY PRODUCTS JOINT STOCK COMPANY	★

Source: Viet Nam Institute of Directors.

Table 9.3:   Viet Nam—Top 30 Publicly Listed Companies in the ASEAN Corporate Governance Scorecard Based on 2019 Total Score
(alphabetical order by stock code)

Stock Code	Company Name	
BSI	BIDV SECURITIES JOINT STOCK COMPANY	
BVH	BAOVIET HOLDINGS	
BVS	BAO VIET SECURITIES JOINT STOCK COMPANY	
CTD	COTECCONS CONSTRUCTION JOINT STOCK COMPANY	
CTG	VIET NAM JOINT STOCK COMMERCIAL BANK FOR INDUSTRY AND TRADE	
DGW	DIGIWORLD CORP	
DHG	DHG PHARMACEUTICAL JOINT STOCK COMPANY	
DMC	DOMESCO MEDICAL IMPORT EXPORT JOINT STOCK CORP	
FPT	FPT CORPORATION	
GMD	GEMADEPT CORPORATION	
HCM	HO CHI MINH CITY SECURITIES CORPORATION	
MBB	MILITARY COMMERCIAL JOINT STOCK BANK	
NVL	NOVALAND GROUP	
PAN	THE PAN GROUP JOINT STOCK COMPANY	
PGD	PETRO VIET NAM LOW PRESSURE GAS DISTRIBUTION JOINT STOCK COMPANY	
SAB	SAIGON BEER – ALCOHOL – BEVERAGE CORPORATION	
SBT	THANH THANH CONG - BIEN HOA JOINT STOCK COMPANY	
SCR	SAI GON THUONG TIN REAL ESTATE JOINT STOCK COMPANY	
SHS	SAIGON - HANOI SECURITIES JSC	
SSI	SSI SECURITIES CORPORATION	
STK	CENTURY SYNTHETIC FIBER CORPORATION	
TCB	VIETNAM TECHNOLOGICAL AND COMMERCIAL JOINT STOCK BANK	
TCM	THANH CONG TEXTILE GARMENT INVESTMENT TRADING JOINT STOCK COMPANY	
TNG	TNG INVESTMENT AND TRADING JSC	
TRA	TRAPHACO JOINT STOCK COMPANY	
VCB	JOINT STOCK COMMERCIAL BANK FOR FOREIGN TRADE OF VIET NAM	
VJC	VIETJET AVIATION JOINT STOCK COMPANY	
VND	VNDIRECT SECURITIES CORPORATION	
VNM	VIET NAM DAIRY PRODUCTS JOINT STOCK COMPANY	★
VPB	VIET NAM PROSPERITY JOINT STOCK COMMERCIAL BANK	

Source: Viet Nam Institute of Directors.

References

Asian Development Bank (ADB). 2013. *ASEAN Corporate Governance Scorecard Country Reports and Assessments 2012–2013*. Manila. May.

ADB. 2014. *ASEAN Corporate Governance Scorecard Country Reports and Assessments 2014*. Manila. June.

———. 2016. *ASEAN Corporate Governance Scorecard Country Reports and Assessments 2013–2014*. Manila. July.

———. 2017. *ASEAN Corporate Governance Scorecard Country Reports and Assessments 2015*. Manila. October.

Organisation for Economic Co-operation and Development. 2004. OECD Principles of Corporate Governance, 2004. Paris.

www.ingramcontent.com/pod-product-compliance
Lightning Source LLC
Chambersburg PA
CBHW061221270326
41926CB00032B/4797